WEAVING THROUGH THE LABYRINTH

Emerging from a Traumatic Brain Injury

To Roni & Gregor,
Never give up....!
ginger

WEAVING THROUGH THE LABYRINTH

Emerging from a Traumatic Brain Injury

A Memoir

Ginger Theisen

"Walking the labyrinth is a spiritual discipline that invites us to trust the path, to surrender to the many turns our lives take, and to walk through the confusion, the fear, the anger, and grief that we cannot avoid experiencing as we live our earthly lives."

Rev. Dr. Lauren Artress

PLATTE RIVER
PUBLISHING

Published by

Platte River Publishing

Omaha, Nebraska

ISBN: 978-1-7356484-0-8 (paperback edition)
       978-1-7356484-1-5 (eBook edition)

BISAC codes:
BIO026000 BIOGRAPHY & AUTOBIOGRAPHY / Personal Memoirs
BIO022000 BIOGRAPHY & AUTOBIOGRAPHY / Women
BIO017000 BIOGRAPHY & AUTOBIOGRAPHY / Medical *(incl. Patients)*

Cover and logo design and author photo by Angel Stottle
Cover photo by Christine Lesiak
Interior photographs provided by Ginger Theisen

Printed in the United States of America by

Lincoln, Nebraska

To my sweet dear son, Nolan.

Acknowledgments

Through these last seven years since the horse accident, I have been on a journey of healing and self-discovery enriched by the love and generosity of my family, friends and new acquaintances.

I want to thank my family; Nolan, Mark, Trish, John and Robin, for always being there through all the twists and turns during my recovery.

When I was able to physically write a couple of words and eventually compose a sentence, I started to keep a journal about what I was experiencing. This evolved into the first chapter of this book which helped me work through this significant event in my life. I am incredibly grateful to my therapist Becky, who helped guide me through it, encouraging me to continue writing which opened up and connected parts of my life that had been blocked after the traumatic brain injury.

To steer me through the process of turning this into a book, I want to thank Doug Erlandson for his wise and knowledgeable advice and helping me pull this together. Also, many thanks to the following people who helped get this book to the finish line: Trish Billotte for proofreading, Fr. Thomas at St. Benedict Center in Schuyler, Nebraska for giving us access to their labyrinth, Christine Lesiak for taking the photographs of me walking the labyrinth, my niece, Angel Stottle for designing the cover of the book and Dr. William Thorell and Dr. Richard Legge for proofing the medical terminology. Also, I want to thank Mikala Harden, his company Say Hi There and the photographer, Nate Gasaway, for the drone shot of the labyrinth from the St. Benedict Center video.

1

Pieces to the Puzzle

On a beautiful warm September day in 2013, I went horseback riding on the lovely grounds of Mt. Michael Abbey, with one of the Benedictine monks, Brother Mel. We had just started out on our ride when my horse slipped and fell, taking me with her, all 1,350 pounds, landing right on top of me. The horse got up, but I did not.

Eventually, family and friends told me the rest of the story. I was taken to the emergency room at a hospital in the nearby city of Omaha, Nebraska. It is quite a strange experience to find out much later on that you have no memory of what happened. I was in pretty bad shape with a traumatic brain injury. They decided to put me in an induced coma, expecting me to come out of it in a couple of days. Several days went by, and the tests showed I had no brain activity. The doctors told my family I was not coming back.

Based on this information, my family was asked to make a big decision, whether or not to keep me plugged in to the equipment keeping me alive. In fact, I had just created a medical power of attorney a couple of months earlier, appointing my son to serve in that capacity. In the document, I specifically addressed the situation I was now in. I did not want to be kept alive if there were no positive signs I was going to make it. This is not an easy decision for anyone to make, and I still cannot fathom how heavily this must have weighed on him, my family, and friends. This all unfolded in a very short period of time from my son hearing I was in an induced "managed" coma to learning I was likely not going to wake up. Given the doctor's newfound grim prognosis and my wishes to not be kept in a vegetative state, my son decided to take me off life support.

The day before this was going to happen, Nolan had let my closest friends know, garnering all kinds of emotional responses. He, along with family, my niece Angel, who was flying in from Chicago, and friends who were close by came to the hospital to say their goodbyes, all of them thinking this was it. However, when Angel was still in flight to Omaha, I gently squeezed the finger of Dr. Matanaj, the neurosurgeon, the faintest of signs for him to witness some activity, indicating that there was still hope for me. This small, simple gesture was a game-changer. The doctor firmly believed I should be kept on life support, giving me a chance. He did not need to be told twice.

From that point, it was a slow and unsure emergence out of the coma. My son and niece wondered openly how far I would actually come, where the progress would stop. None of the doctors had an answer—no one knew. But sure enough, day by day, there were small encouraging improvements—from squeezing to making tiny movements with my right hand, my left foot, my right foot, and eyes tracking from side to side. A miracle was unfolding before everyone around me. I have no memory of any of this.

Everyone was watching to see how I would come out of it; the signs continued to be positive. Lots of things started happening, and big decisions had to be made quickly. I had several broken bones on the right side of my face and a broken clavicle. The surgery for my face was done pretty quickly after I came out of the coma, so it was a risky decision for my son to make, but it was definitely the right one. The plastic surgeon, Dr. Bhuller, repaired the broken bones around my right eye, basically putting them back together again.

One would think coming out of a coma is like flipping a switch back on and—presto— you are back among the living. But for me or anyone who has had brain trauma, it does not work that way. Essentially, it scrambles the neurons in your brain, and you have to figure out how to unscramble them. It is not a simple or easy process, but it's amazing how it can and does happen.

The brain is complex and capable of healing in ways that are remarkable. My thought processes in the beginning of this adventure came back in snippets of awareness, quite disjointed and frenetic. I was still trying to figure out details of where I was and how I had gotten there. My sense of time was nonexistent.

Instinctually I knew my focus was to find out how and what was needed to help me return to this world. Some things started to come back more easily than others, but I had to relearn pretty much everything. I could usually visualize what a conversation was about, but the part of connecting it all together was challenging. The social filter was nonexistent, so sometimes I was very direct or blunt when I was able to respond. Add to the mix how to pronounce a word or its correct spelling was overwhelming at times. All of these things take time and a lot of patience to sink into your brain again. I am living proof. It will and does come back.

Since the accident, I have been in recovery, improving in big and small ways, always surrounded by loving, supportive family and friends. Now I am ready to tell you the story about the journey I have been on, discovering who I was and who I am now.

Two years after the accident, I started to write about the seemingly uncharted territory I was navigating through to get back to "me." Updates in italics were added as I regained more awareness and understood the details of what was going on. A small amount of editing has been done, but mainly, this is a clear reflection of my thought process and point of view. I hope this gives the reader a glimpse into what it was like to recover from a traumatic brain injury.

This is my story from the beginning.

I remember two faces looking at me. The first one was Abbot Michael in deep prayer. Somehow I knew the prayer was for me and that the situation was not good. The second face I saw had a warm, motherly glow. It was Angel, who was very pregnant at the time; she was smiling at me. I do not know when these took place, but it was at the hospital because that is when they both came to see me.

Two years later, Angel told me when they decided to move me from Creighton Hospital to the Madonna Rehabilitation Hospital in Lincoln, she asked me if I wanted to be back in Paris instead and I quickly nodded, "yes" and shot her a look that was indicative of "me." It was a place I had been many times before and loved it. My response showed her a lot because a week earlier I had just come out of a coma and had plastic surgery done on my face. But this response was a really good sign; several parts of my brain were functioning and intact.

This was around the time I was ready to hear more stories about what happened while I was at Creighton Hospital. My family and friends told me that when I was in the coma, they spent time talking to me, reading articles from the New York Times *and verses from the Bible and looking at photos, describing what we were doing, hoping to engage me. Being surrounded by this kind of love, prayers, and support is amazingly powerful and had to be a part of bringing me out of the coma. There were people from all over the world praying for me, some of them I have never met. My family told me that when I came out of the coma, I was aware and coherent, having brief conversations with them. I do not remember any of this.*

Then I was wheeled down a hallway with a nurse next to me. I told her my feet were cold. I think they were taking me to a vehicle to be transported somewhere else. The next thing I remember was lying on something, hearing the sound of tires hitting pavement. I felt movement. It seemed like I was by myself; I had no sense of time.

Nolan told me this was when I had been released from Creighton Hospital and transported to Madonna Rehabilitation Hospital in Lincoln, Nebraska. He and Angel were in my VW Jetta following the ambulance and were there when they checked me in. I have no recollection of this.

Maybe this memory was soon after they had checked me in, but I remember lying on a bed in a room. People came in to check on me. I followed the light and saw it was coming from the window. Looking further, I saw a street with trees and parked cars. Then it began to dawn on me I had no idea where I was or why I was there. No sounds, just glimpses of movements, visually perceiving what was around me in that room.

I do not remember much about the first couple of weeks at Madonna. Much later on, my friend Kim told me she had visited me soon after I had arrived. The nurses asked me who that was. I did not respond right away. Kim was about to speak for me, but the nurses asked her to wait for me to say something. After a few minutes I said, "This is my friend Kim." She started crying and called Shelley on her cell phone and handed it to me. I said, "Hi Shelley Bell," my nickname for her. They were both crying at this point. I still do not remember any of it.

Pieces of reality continued to come back to me in brief snippets. I was moved into another room. I think this was when things started to click in my brain with more clarity. I was aware of my daily schedule, which meant a female nurse's aide helped me bathe, brush my teeth, and get dressed in a pair of loose pants and top. One of the priests came by to give me communion right before they brought my breakfast.

Next was physical and speech therapy. I always felt better when I went to the gym to work out.

I have a vivid memory of being in a small room with the speech therapist, who was showing me images on a piece of paper, asking me to choose one set and describe them. The whole thing seemed odd to me. I knew in my mind what they were, but I did not know how to verbalize it and got frustrated. My mind seemed to travel to distant places outside that room.

A couple times a week I attended group sessions with the counselor. It was probably my first meeting when she explained to the rest of the group that the reason my voice sounded different was because I still had the tracheostomy tube in. This was taken out later at Madonna.

I never thought about why I had the tracheostomy tube or G-tube; they were just there, attached to my body. I was not clear about why until I saw the doctors at Creighton Hospital two months later.

Other than the staff coming into my room to check on me, I know my brother John and Robin were there several times. By this point, it had started to sink in that something bad had happened to me involving a horse. Soon after that, I distinctly remember seeing my son, Nolan, which made me very happy. I remember looking down at my hands and asking him to please bring me a pair of fingernail clippers and some of my CDs, because there was a player in the room. Then I told him I was never going to ride horses again.

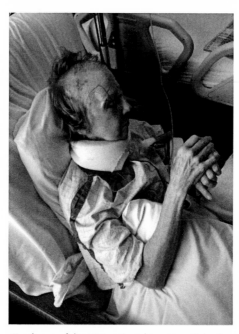

Fresh out of the ICU at Creighton Hospital, after twelve days, they moved me to a room in the transitional care unit, unplugged from all the equipment that had kept me alive while I was in a coma. The plastic surgery had been done that morning to repair the broken bones around my right eye and cheek. This is how my son, Nolan, described what had happened the day he took this photo, twelve days after the accident on September 12, 2013.

He had been at the hospital the whole time and checked on me at Madonna until he flew back to Myrtle Beach, South Carolina, where he was living. To me, seeing him that day at Madonna was the first time I saw him.

Slowly this newfound reality continued to become more clear, and I began to feel like I was a part of the world around me. Things were still overwhelming, scary, and humorous, sometimes at the same time, as I was figuring out the big picture of this familiar life I had lived before the accident happened.

Dr. LaHolt always checked on me early around 6 A.M. I vividly remember him telling me one morning it would help me to heal more quickly if I sat up in the chair straighter and did not sleep curled up in a ball. Up to that point, I had been holding everything in my body so tightly together, like a fetal position, especially when I slept. The whole concept struck me, and it was a profound moment, realizing that was how I had been protecting my whole self, probably for weeks, starting at the hospital. This was a big step. It helped me open up and feel like I needed to move forward on every level.

I started to know and recognize who was coming to visit me consistently. Some were friends and relatives I had not seen since I lived in Lincoln thirty years ago. It was quite an experience to talk on the phone the first couple of times—kind of trippy, for sure. I remember talking to my cousin, Pete; my friend, Mandy; and Nolan. I was not yet fully capable of having a conversation on the phone, so they were brief, but it felt so good to hear their voices.

Five-and-a-half years later, Mandy told me I sounded like a robot, slowly answering some of her questions. She realized then I had a long road ahead of me. And Nolan, told me he was shocked, talking to me on the phone the first time that I could actually converse with him!

A couple of weeks into my stay at Madonna, things came back more frequently and for longer periods of time. I'm not sure exactly when this occurred, but I had a very clear, powerful memory of being in a place that was definitely not here on earth nor was it a dream. I was surrounded by a deep, rich sense of love embracing me. I felt God's presence and all of my loved ones who have passed on: my sister Diane, my parents, grandparents, and Angel's daughter, Aviana. This place was like a Maxfield Parrish landscape with rich, beautiful colors and lots of trees and hills, all deeply saturated hues that gave me a feeling of joy. I felt happy, at peace and safe, wanting to explore more. I did not see shapes of my loved ones but felt a strong presence.

I was intrigued being in another part of the universe, traveling about, flitting to different places. I was having fun, enjoying this—no sense of time like there is on earth. I felt very comfortable there—deeply loved, not afraid in any way, completely absorbed in this spirit world feeling free, fearless, and fascinated by it all.

It was my sister Diane's presence that was the strongest. She's always been with me in other difficult times, one of the biggest guardian angels watching over me. She's the one who told me to get myself together and go back—it is not my time yet.

I had not completely comprehended how serious my accident was or that I had a traumatic brain injury. It took me weeks to realize why there were incredibly beautiful flowers, cards, and a guardian angel sitting in front of the windowsill in my room. I finally understood they were from people who knew me, sending their love and best wishes to get well soon. When I realized this, a deep sense of emotions filled my heart and mind with warmth and joy once again.

I did not fully understand the depth of caring and loving, supportive words written in those cards and letters until a year later when I opened the small colorful package that contained them. As I read through each one, tears softly flowed down my cheeks.

One night when I was watching television in my room by myself, a commercial with Will Ferrell came on. He was talking about the brand of pickup trucks lined up behind him, and there were three actual horses standing next to him, of all things. The way he was acting and the dialogue he used was familiar to me and so hilarious. I started laughing out loud as tears ran down my cheeks. That was the first time I remember actually laughing. Then memories flooded back in waves: I was a visual effects producer! I had worked with him on the film *The Other Guys*. Amazingly, a big piece of the puzzle fell into place at that moment. With complete clarity, I rediscovered a part of my life I loved and deeply cherished.

At some point, either before or after I had this revelation, my very dear friends, Erika and Richard, flew out from Los Angeles to see me when I was at Madonna. Erika and I had worked together at Industrial Light and Magic (ILM). I remember bits and pieces of their visit. Later, after I was released, Erika told me when they came into my room, the nurse asked me who they were. With a big smile I said, "Erika and Richard." I especially remember Erika's reaction—she had a huge smile.

I went on line a year later and found out the commercial I saw was for Anchorman 2: The Legend Continues, *released in the fall of 2013.*

When I could walk on my own, I was allowed to be more independent and sometimes took walks around the whole facility. It was an amazing feeling to explore on my own. I found Father Stephen's office, and he gave me a tour of the area where the children were. An incredibly deep sense of compassion and empathy came over me. I discovered the chapel and often went there to sit and pray. I remember walking through the area that was set up like a kitchen where I was taught some basic skills, which seemed a bit foreign to me at that time.

On the walk back to my room, I passed by a large fish aquarium and was fascinated by the activity going on in there. I was also aware of the time when my friend Cathy stopped by to visit. It just seemed like part of my routine to walk up to the front entrance and wait for her. My friends, Kim, Shelley, and Larry, stopped by to visit me several times, too. I remember seeing Melissa and my cousin, Martha. I was being more like myself now, socially engaged in full conversations that made sense to me.

I do not remember much about discussions regarding my release from Madonna other than possibly moving me to a halfway house to live, but I chose to go back to my brother Mark's house. It was probably too soon for me to be back functioning in the world again, but my insurance company decided they were not going to cover any more of the costs. They clearly did not fully understand all the effects brain trauma has on a person. But that was the reality of the situation. Thank goodness my family and friends were there to guide me through this major transition I was about to embark on.

It was not until I visited Madonna the second time, two-and-a-half years later, that I was in the brain trauma unit. Some of the other patients in that unit did not make eye contact or have a conversation with me the two months I was there. Now I understood why.

My friends Judi and Chris stopped by and brought me gifts the day before I was released. I told them I was going home the next day and did not need them. I do not remember saying this, just the thought of how generous they were to bring me gifts. My social skills were not completely working yet. At the same time, my financial advisor, Jack, stopped by and brought me some fries and a hamburger from Don & Millie's. The smell wafted down the hallway, and two nurses came in to find out what was going on. They just smiled. For me, it was like a symphony of sensations firing off at the same time. This was my first taste of real food after months of a bland hospital diet. It was amazing.

The next day I said my goodbyes to the wonderful doctors, nurses, and staff who had taken such good care of me during my stay at Madonna. One of the nurses helped me put on the clothes that Mark had brought. As we walked out the front entrance, I could feel all my senses kicking into high gear.

When I was released from Madonna, I remember packing up the cards and the bag with my riding chaps, boots, and the ripped up jeans I wore when the accident happened. For some reason, the angel from Abbot Michael and the sweatshirt from Shelley, along with some other things, did not get packed. Honestly, I did not know this until I visited Madonna for the first time several months later. They were in a box where they had put other things I had left in the room. Evidently, this happened a lot.

Five-and-a-half years later, Abbot Michael vividly remembered the small angel he got for me when I was in a coma that he put on the stand near my bed. A day later it disappeared but showed up the following day with a piece of scotch tape around one arm. Nolan suggested to Abbot Michael he may want to replace it. But that angel was there when he watched my eyes slowly track the nurses in my room a couple days before I came out of the coma. At this point, Abbot Michael said that broken angel was part of the miracle; she had absorbed my brokenness so I could begin to heal. He still gets goosebumps when he tells this story. He did give me a new angel before I left the hospital and was sent with my things to Madonna. This angel now sits in front of my large north window, quietly watching over me.

After we got to Omaha, Mark took me to my favorite restaurant for lunch, M's Pub in the Old Market. I was a bit overwhelmed being out in public, but I definitely remembered this place. I knew that I liked the Greek sandwich with a glass of dry French sauvignon blanc, and Mark ordered that for me. I was only able to eat a little bit and have a sip of the wine, but I sensed it was normal and that I had done things like this many times before.

Then we drove to Mark's house where I was living when I moved back to Nebraska from New York City a year before the accident. We were just about to turn into the driveway when a van pulled up behind us, delivering a beautiful orchid from my dear friends, Chuck and Anne Trimble. What a wonderful welcoming home gift. When we pulled into the garage, I felt the floodgates beginning to open, accelerating my reentry back into the real world.

The house was very familiar to me. He parked the car in the garage next to my car. As I walked into the kitchen, things started clicking in. I knew the steps on the other side led up to my bedroom. I did not remember learning how to navigate steps at Madonna, but I was okay going up them. Right away, I felt comfortable and safe being back in this house.

Walking into my bedroom the first time felt familiar, too. My clothes and shoes were neatly put away in the closet. Suddenly, I had a new sense of freedom, realizing it was up to me to select a piece of clothing to wear for the day. There were moments when certain clothes triggered some memories, connecting me to places and events I had experienced before. Figuring out how to do all the typical things in a normal daily routine was now my responsibility.

As I began to reorient myself, it seemed like so many things were rapidly clicking in. My *New York Times* newspapers were stacked in a pile next to my MacBook sitting on the same desk next to the kitchen where I had left it. Outside, Mark had watered the little garden I had planted that summer. With the mild weather, the fresh herbs and strawberries were still producing, keeping the rabbits happy. These were all significant things my brother had kept. Whether he realized it at the time, a lot of this brought back more clarity of who I was before.

My dear friends Mandy and Jim had made plans to come out and see me, thinking I would still be at Madonna. The day before they arrived, I had just gotten back to Mark's house. Even though it was late in the evening and past my bedtime, I felt it was important to go to the airport to pick them up with Mark. This sparked more memories as we drove out there because I realized that I had taken this route several times before.

Talk about God's timing. They had arrived just in time to help me adjust during my first week at the house. Since Mark was at work during the day, this was a pivotal point in this early stage of my recovery. I didn't realize it then, but I was not ready to be by myself during the day. It was such a huge blessing to be around them, sparking more pieces of the puzzle to fall into place.

They helped put together a huge dinner on Sunday to celebrate my homecoming with family and a small group of friends. It was an incredible experience for me to be around so much joy, sitting at the table with these loved ones and enjoying a meal together. I could not eat that much, but cherished every moment.

The next morning, they left to fly back to California. I vividly remember the looks on their faces, one of worry and concern. My ability to have a full conversation was slowly improving, but I could barely read a complete sentence let alone a paragraph in the newspaper at this point. This was when it began to sink in. Clearly, I had a long road ahead.

Much later, Nolan told me that when I had come out of the coma, the nurses were testing and teaching me movements by voice command, mimicking how to put one finger in front of my nose and touch it, following the movement with my eyes to see if I had eye/hand coordination. I could not figure out how to do this seemingly simple task. At this point, he was really worried about my ability to function again on all levels.

Mandy and Jim gave me a lovely book about Alaska called *Surviving the Island of Grace*. She picked this one out hoping it would bring back memories of an important and significant time in my life. Indeed, it did bring back a lot of those memories. With more clarity I remembered specific events during the years I lived there and commercial fished with Ken, my son's father.

Mark made arrangements for a nurse and speech therapist to come to the house twice a week to work with me after they left. The nurse was worried about me walking up and down the steps, so she watched me do this to make sure I was capable of doing this on my own. The speech therapist started the sessions out with sounding out a list of words, then spelling them. This method definitely helped improve my vocabulary. After a couple of weeks, I was able to read portions of an article in the newspaper by myself.

Mark also set up appointments at Creighton Hospital with the doctors who had treated me after the accident. John and Robin took me to see them. Walking into that hospital and the sounds, smells, and activities sparked a lot of emotions, but not much clarity as to why until much later. The first appointment was with Dr. Bergmann, the orthopedic trauma surgeon. He checked my broken clavicle on the right side and was pleased to see how well it had healed and gave me exercises to strengthen my shoulder. Next was an MRI. It felt a bit surreal to slide into this narrow space with loud sounds and lights flashing, but I got through it.

All the other appointments were in another part of the hospital. They put us in one room so each doctor could come in individually to examine me. At this point, I was really overwhelmed, trying to understand and absorb what was going on and being discussed. I'm not sure who came in first, but I think it was Dr. Wagner, the trauma and critical care surgeon. He showed me how to keep the area around the G-tube clean. When Dr. Bhuller, the plastic surgeon, walked in, I remember his smile and the inquisitive look on his face. I am pretty sure he was the only one who asked me if I remembered him. I told him, no, I did not. No doubt, they must have been a bit blown away by how far I was in my recovery since coming out of the coma two months earlier.

It took me a while to fully comprehend that these were the doctors who had kept me alive, repairing the broken bones in my face and putting in the tracheostomy and the G-tube. It was a strange experience to feel a sense of being physically present, aware of things going on around me but not feeling completely there. I knew my brain was trying to absorb and engage but had a limited capacity to do so. I instinctually felt so grateful to all of them—the nurses and the staff—for what they had done for me.

The G-tube was put in through my abdominal wall into the stomach so I could receive nutrients while I was in the coma at Creighton Hospital. About four months later, Dr. Wagner had the resident doctor literally yank the tube out. I will always have a nice scar from it.

There were things I wanted to tell the doctors that day, especially the loud ringing sound in my head that was constant, keeping me awake most of the time. I was aware of it when I was at Madonna, but I was not able to express or verbalize what was going on. I just knew something was seriously wrong.

When I was at Mark's house, I always had some kind of background sound on to lessen the loud ringing I heard in my head. The problem finally got figured out six months later by another neurosurgeon.

There were glimpses of a reality I recognized and remembered, but they were in snippets, disjointed and nonlinear, and I was figuring out how to connect them. An odd, trippy experience when things come back randomly, realizing I did them in the same way as before the accident.

Each day, I was aware of connecting more parts of my collective memory to untangle those neurons in my brain, as more revelations were uncovered. I started using my computer, opening up the notebooks organized on the desk next to it, glancing at the script titled *Crazy Horse* with notes written on different pages and earmarked, a pile of signed release forms for the Crazy Horse Ride, lots of memories were flooding back with more clarity. This complex life I had lived before was quickly emerging. Processing all of this had to be done in small steps until I was capable of piecing it all together again. Instinctually I sensed it could not be done at the fast-paced level I had worked at before.

After a couple of weeks at Mark's house, he took me grocery shopping at Whole Foods. This was the first time shopping since I left Madonna. We went on a Saturday when there were lots of people rushing around with their carts. It did not take long before I just froze and stood still, not really knowing what to do. Everyone was moving too fast. The whole experience was certainly overwhelming, plus I did not know what I wanted, so Mark helped me pick out prepared foods he knew I liked before.

Around the same time, no doubt risky, Mark had me drive my Jetta, a stick not an automatic, to the gas station and grocery store near his house. I had frequently gone to the same places before the accident. I do not know how or what sparked that memory, but I knew exactly how to get there. Honestly, to have me actually drive was probably not something any of my doctors would have advised at this point in my recovery, but it definitely pushed me to be more independent being able to drive on my own.

I lost a lot of weight since the accident and knew it was important to gain it back. I really did not have much of an appetite, and my sense of taste and smell was there, but not as much as before. Doing some kind of physical activity like taking a walk or eventually going to the gym would get my appetite going in the beginning for brief periods of time. I realized early on that these were the things that triggered an awareness that I was hungry. It also helped to cook and have meals with friends and family, not by myself.

When my son visited a year after the accident, we were listening to a show on NPR talking about french toast. Just those words brought back a flood of vivid memories of my mother making it for me and of my making it for Nolan when he was growing up. It was all rapidly firing in my mind as I realized it was one of my favorite dishes to have for breakfast. I made it the next morning with Nolan as my sous chef. It was delicious. These kinds of connections just seemed to click in my brain randomly, like this one.

One of the other things that had not crossed my mind until I was at Mark's house for a couple of weeks was that when I looked in the mirror, I realized that my hair on the right side of my head was a lot shorter and uneven. It never occurred to me when I was at Madonna to think about washing and styling my hair but I was now beginning to be more aware of how I looked. At this point, I just thought someone had given me a bad haircut. The reality of why my hair looked like that slowly began to sink in through the stories friends and family were telling me.

Now I understood that when I arrived in the emergency room at Creighton Hospital, the reason they had shaved the right side of my head was to open up and release the pressure in the cranial area that was caused by the weight of the horse landing on my head. This procedure helped save my life. Mark set up an appointment with my hairdresser, Crystal, for the following week. She had cut my hair previously and knew about the accident. He kindly drove me to the first couple of appointments until I could drive there by myself. It took a good year and a half until my hair grew to the same length on both sides.

In April of 2019, I went to Europe to visit Nolan. He told me about a photo he had taken of me in the hospital with my head shaved and showed me. Wow, a bit of a shock to see myself like that, but I smiled, realizing the significance of how far I had come since that day, five-and-a-half years ago.

After a couple months of speech therapy at Mark's house, I found a similar rehabilitation program like Madonna's at Immanuel Rehabilitation Institute in Omaha. I started the same kind of speech therapy and physical therapy in January of 2014. My dear friends, Anne and Betty, took turns picking me up and driving me out there. This time the speech therapy really clicked for me.

The speech therapist, Sarah, gave me lessons on physically writing and sounding out the answers that gradually increased in complexity. There was always a radio on or some kind of ambient noise in the background, so I was familiar and comfortable working in that kind of environment. She also gave me homework to do at home. I made huge strides during those four months with her. The physical and aqua therapy were also extremely helpful, improving my balance, posture, and overall strength.

Learning how to spell words again was the most challenging. Each day I would read and write with pen and paper, which helped me regain those skills. Sometimes, when I saw an object like a fire hydrant or a convertible car, I knew what it was, but I did not remember the correct word. During the first year, I often felt my mind search for it, but if I could not come up with the correct word, I asked the person who was with me for help. Sometimes, looking at the letters on my keyboard, a word would come back, and I could spell it. No explanation—it just happened. I still get the meaning and spelling of words like "hear" and "here" or "saw" and "say" mixed up. I have a renewed respect for people learning the English language for the first time.

During my speech therapy sessions at Immanuel, I started to write a list of the words I have been relearning on my iPhone with spell check turned off. I still add words to the list, studying it until I have memorized it. A crossword puzzle book is also a good exercise. My friend Cathy, picked one up for me at the grocery store after I left

Madonna. Now I do the mini-crossword puzzle in the New York Times.

My brothers and Nolan helped me go through my bills and showed me how to write checks again. I had to relearn how to write my legal name, too. One of the many bills to pay was to the Volunteer Fire Department in Waterloo, Nebraska. They were the first responders who took me to the emergency room at Creighton Hospital. I have absolutely no memory of this.

In the spring of 2015, I was on a flight from Omaha to Dallas to visit my friend Kristie and her family in Austin. When we landed, I was waiting to get off the plane and saw this man in front of me wearing a sweatshirt with the words "Waterloo Volunteer Fire Department" written in large letters. I asked him if he was with that fire department. He smiled and said yes. We struck up a conversation, and I told him about my accident when I was riding a horse at Mt. Michael in September of 2013. The look of surprise and disbelief came over his face and his wife's. He was one of those first responders who took me to Creighton Hospital in the ambulance. I shook his hand and thanked him.

There were several other things that needed my attention after I got back to Mark's house. Besides bills to pay, there was a receipt from the dry cleaners with my name on it. I had no memory of this, but the date was a week before the accident, so the clothes had been there for several months. When I went to pick them up the next week, my shirts were there, waiting for me. The company I had my health insurance with cancelled me in December of 2013, four months after the accident. Given everything that happened since then, the only way I could get insurance was through the Affordable Care Act. Thank goodness it was an option to still get coverage. Nolan got me signed up with a new healthcare plan that started the beginning of January.

A core group of friends and family kept me actively involved. Once a week, Brother Mel picked me up to go out to Mt. Michael for noon prayers and lunch. We would read out loud something from the newspaper and a couple of pages from the book, *Proof of Heaven*, by Eben Alexander. Every other weekend, Cathy's husband, John, picked me up after he got off work on Fridays, and I spent the weekend with them in Lincoln. Angel, her husband Matt, and their son, Von, moved back to Omaha, close to Mark's house, and we often took walks together when the weather permitted it. My friend, Erika, came back to visit, and we had many conversations about the visual effects work she had just finished. In the spring, John and Robin were back from Arizona. They often came down from Norfolk for a nice delicious lunch with some of the steaks or hamburgers they brought with them. My friend from New York City, Julie, stopped by with her sister when she came back to see family. All these visits brought back memories of experiences I had shared with them, helping me piece together with more knowledge and certainty that I was still me, the same person I was before the accident happened.

The author of Proof of Heaven *is a neurosurgeon who wrote about going through a serious medical situation that put him in a coma and his experience in the spirit world. It was striking how the memory of mine was so similar to his.*

Unfolding around me were the film projects I was involved in: the feature film, *Crazy Horse*, the documentary on the Crazy Horse Ride, and the short film, *Rebecca's Story*, with the Witness Project in Guyana. Soon after the accident, the number of people who wanted to know what was going on kept growing, so Nolan set up a space on Caring Bridge where he posted updates on my condition. This was how my friends, relatives, and colleagues on the film projects and the industry were updated with what was going on.

A year later, Nolan told me people had written messages to both of us on Caring Bridge. When I read them a couple of months later, it was incredibly emotional. The words of support, encouragement, and prayers gave me such a deep sense of gratitude and feeling so deeply loved.

Every step I made, they were there, patiently waiting for me to get back on track. It took a while for those projects to sink in and to ascertain exactly what stage they were in before the accident. It got more challenging and complex as I began to regain the ability to verbally describe and express my thoughts. As things evolved with more clarity, especially the film and the documentary, I began to sense the drive and excitement I had before coming back.

As these fragments of my ability to function as a visual effects (VFX) producer again were coming back, I was discovering more about who I had been before. There were photos on my digital camera and iPhone I had taken on film sets after leaving ILM, sparking more clarity and specific memories of being at those places with people I had worked with. The combination of that and listening to my CD's and music on my iPhone slowly triggered a more expansive awareness of who I was and the things I had experienced.

A year later when I was driving to Lincoln to visit friends, I had music playing from the song list I had put together on my iPhone before the accident happened. For some reason when the song, Vertigo, *by U2 came on., it reached a part of my brain that brought back a bunch of memories. They were vivid ones of me driving up a mountain outside the town of Smithers in British Columbia. I was going to the film set for* Eight Below, *the first project since I left ILM, freelancing as the VFX producer. We were shooting on the top of a mountain in the dead of winter. I often listened to U2's* How to Dismantle an Atomic Bomb, *and that was one of the songs that got me energized. Ready to start another day full of new adventures shooting exterior scenes in the freezing cold Canadian winter.*

In February of 2014, the loud whooshing sound in my head was not going away, affecting my sleep and overall ability to focus on those projects. I made appointments with all the doctors I saw before the accident, and only one of them, my internist, Dr. Shehan, listened with his stethoscope to pinpoint where it was coming from. He was the first doctor to tell me the left eye was red and bloodshot. I knew it was not good. He sent me to Dr. Thedinger, an ear, nose and throat specialist, who agreed there was something going on, but not critical. So given that assessment, he sent me to Dr. Thorell, a neurosurgeon at the University of Nebraska Medical Center. But it took four weeks before I got in to see him. Neither doctor realized how serious my situation was.

By mid-March, my left eye got worse, making my vision cloudy, almost double, and I had to stop driving. I went back to my eye doctor who recommended cataract surgery that might solve the redness in my left eye. I just wanted to get my vision working again and trusted his suggestion and scheduled the surgery for mid-May.

So many things were happening, sometimes all at once, but I learned to deal with them in more simple ways so as not to get too overwhelmed. In the beginning of my recovery, I was more vulnerable, easily shedding tears when I heard or watched emotional stories being told even on the radio, a film, or a show on television. The first couple of years, when I heard emergency vehicles, I started praying for everyone involved in that emergency situation. I still have those feelings now, but not quite as sensitive as they were in the beginning. It also takes a while to feel comfortable being around a lot of people. For me, this has been part of the process of healing from the physical and emotional parts of my recovery.

On April 10, 2014, the day of my birthday, I had my first appointment with Dr. Thorell. I remember the day vividly. On this perfect warm spring day, I spent the morning outside, pulling weeds and watering the garden. With a nice cup of espresso, I sat on the deck to take in the lush green surroundings. I was happy and content to have this quiet peaceful moment and hoped this doctor would be the one to tell me there was a simple solution to reduce the loud sound. My friend Betty picked me up, and we chatted on the way there about this lovely spring day.

As soon as Dr. Thorell walked in, he got right to the point. He had already gone through my charts and MRI from Creighton Hospital. He showed me on the screen the MRI scan and took one look of my bloodshot eye. He knew exactly what it was: I had a carotid cavernous fistula. He went on to explain this had happened when I had the accident but had not shown up on the MRI. Usually, people who have this problem either have a stroke or lose their vision. I sat there stunned, in disbelief; after seeing all the other doctors, he nailed the problem in less than fifteen minutes.

The cataract surgery would have further complicated the situation and made it worse. Thank goodness it had been scheduled after my appointment with Dr. Thorell. He told me to wait at least six months, so I rescheduled it for October of 2014.

The next week I went in for an angiogram. This is a complex, delicate procedure that involves putting a long, narrow tube into my femoral artery and navigating it into the arteries that carry blood to the brain. Through this tube, contrast dye is injected while filming the flow of the contrast using digital x-ray cameras. The images were shown in real time on a large screen in the angiography suite. When Dr. Thorell pinpointed the spot where the injury (pseudoaneurysm) was located, it confirmed his diagnosis; I had a carotid cavernous fistula in the carotid artery as it traversed my skull from the neck to the brain. The fistula was caused by the accident seven months ago.

A week and a half later I had the surgery done. Dr. Thorell used the same procedure, but this time with a specialized instrument that threaded together thin strips of platinum, closing up the large hole that had formed. I will be forever grateful to Dr. Thorell for saving me. It is so important to never give up until all avenues are evaluated and a solution is figured out.

When family and friends found out about my diagnosis, they were surprised how serious it was because they knew my left eye had been bloodshot when I was at Madonna, seven months earlier.

Both film projects were moving ahead. My friend and colleague, Timon, flew out to show me his rough cut of the documentary on the Crazy Horse Ride. I was happy to see how far it had progressed and had several conversations about the direction he had taken it and how to proceed going forward. Projects tend to take on a life of their own. Decisions and choices get made with or without your participation. This triggered memories of film projects I had been brought on to finish, but it was usually a situation where I took it over from the producer who had started it, which was never easy. This is how I felt, coming back to the documentary seven months after the accident. But this time I was on the other side, the odd one out. Even though I was ready to be a part of the team again, I knew it had to be done in small steps.

With the other film project, *Crazy Horse*, my friend Chuck, would pick me up and take me out for coffee to read through the script from the beginning, doing a read through, which I remembered doing before on other film projects. When we started, I would slowly read one paragraph at a time and eventually a couple of pages. By the time we finished the script at the end of the summer, the passion I had before the accident was coming back. Slowly, there were glimpses of a renewed sense of purpose that had motivated me before beginning to rise to the surface.

After the surgery to repair the carotid artery in April, I went back to Immanuel to continue my speech and physical therapy. I am not sure how my story got to a reporter for the

Omaha World Herald, but I was interviewed by Erin Grace, who did a lovely story about me. It was on the front page of the July 16, 2014, paper with a photo of me in the pool at Immanuel Rehabilitation Institute. The ability to answer her questions clearly was pretty significant for me. She interviewed some of the doctors at Creighton Hospital and my brother Mark. Some people who read the article called Mt. Michael and asked if they could come out to see where the accident happened. The whole experience seemed a bit surreal.

Holding a king salmon with my dear friend Nance in Petersburg, Alaska, during the spring of 2015, two years into my recovery. I was so happy to be back there visiting her and Don, and to go fishing again was amazing. I spent a good amount of time fighting with that king salmon before pulling it out of the water. Don helped me land it onto the deck of his boat.

During Christmas of 2014 and the spring of 2015, I went to visit my dear friends in California and Alaska. This was my first time seeing them since the accident, and they did not know what to expect or if the Ginger they knew before was showing up. They were happy to see the person I was before. They didn't tell me that until I had been with them for a couple of days, so they treated me like the "normal" Ginger. Whether they realized it or not, it was so important for me to go back to these places and feel as comfortable as I felt the last time I was with them before the accident.

I left California a couple of weeks before the Christmas holiday, and the airports were already full of people traveling out of SFO in San Francisco. My flight was delayed by several hours, so I decided to explore the international terminal where I remembered meeting Nolan years before when he flew back from Budapest, Hungary. There were a lot of things I recognized, especially the gift shop for the San Francisco Museum of Modern Art. The walls around that area had some amazing exhibits of different types of art work on display. As I admired them, a strong vivid sense of magic and curiosity came over me. This was the first time since the accident that I felt that part of me was still there and very much alive.

Often I asked my friends if what I was doing or saying was normal. I realized that my situation was even more challenging because not only was I coming back from a traumatic brain injury, but I was also dealing with getting older at the same time. It was a double whammy. When I told friends that I forgot something, they just laughed and told me they were experiencing that, too.

It takes a while to relearn social skills. Just saying good-bye or see you later was not something I said early in my recovery. Those skills had to be relearned as well. It seemed a little bit awkward if I was the first one to leave, trying to figure out if I was being rude. I was aware of overanalyzing (another word I had to look up and figure out how to spell) the situation. It takes a long time before those skills completely come back. Another was understanding humor. Comments or an explanation with some kind of subtle humor was lost on me; I would take everything literally.

It was probably the combination of dealing with the health issues and getting through my recovery, but after about three years, I do understand humor, even the subtle, dry humor my brothers and Nolan use. Thank goodness I laugh out loud a lot now!

In general, everything seemed to be moving so much faster, and I felt like I was returning to a very different world than the one I remembered before the accident. I also have been relearning how to communicate with people, whether by text, Facebook, Messenger, Instagram, Twitter, there are just too many options, but this is the world we live in now. This process has taken me longer to understand and function with these new social skills and what the proper etiquette is. One of the really perplexing things was when to back out of a parking place if the person in the vehicle next to me was sitting there with the car running. I finally figured out: usually the person was looking at their cell phone, probably reading their email or looking at Facebook.

Other things surfaced as people shared more specific details about what I had gone through. On one of the drives out to Mt. Michael with Brother Mel, he told me about my being in the ICU for several days at Creighton Hospital. I kind of freaked out and got emotional because that reality had not crossed my mind since I had been back at Mark's house. For some reason, having no memory of any of this was still difficult to fathom. Even though he saw the entire accident happen and wanted to tell me, my emotions were so raw at this point I told him, "Not yet." It took a while longer before I was ready to hear exactly how it happened.

Part of what was going through my mind were the memories of growing up riding horses; a part of me was questioning whether or not I remembered how to.

The first time I went over to the barn to visit the horses at Mt. Michael with Brother Mel, the horse I rode the day of the accident, Angel, walked right over to me. Amazingly, I was fine petting her as I stood on the other side of the fence. The next year, Angel started slipping and falling more frequently. They took her into the veterinarian to find out what the problem was. He discovered the horse had a rare neurological disease called equine protozoal myeloencephalitis or EPM, caused by an animal bite, usually from an opossum. It seriously affects the horse's balance, which is why the horse fell on that gravel road we were riding on, causing her rear end to slam my head into those small pieces of rock.

Later that year, I donated my riding chaps and helmet to Mt. Michael to be used by the youth attending their summer camps.

This was about the same time Father John, one of the monks at Mt. Michael, told me he had been working in the garden when the accident happened. When he saw me lying on the ground, not really moving, he came over and held on to me until the ambulance arrived. He described the situation: there was a look of shock on my face, my shirt had ripped open, and there was some blood coming out of my mouth. For some reason, I was ready to hear his story but not Brother Mel's.

So far, the most emotional story was the one John and Robin told me when I was in Arizona during Christmas and New Year's in 2015. When I was at Creighton Hospital the night before, they were going to have the equipment unplugged. Mark, John, Robin, and Nolan were in my hospital room with Abbott Michael. One of the seven sacraments in the Catholic Church is the Anointing of the

Sick. This was what Abbot Michael did for me when I was still in a coma. Nolan, who was crying at this point, held the holy oil as Abbot Michael laid his hands over me with the oil to give me strength to heal. They were facing what they thought at the time was an inevitable reality, I was not coming back. I was stunned. I just sat there and had to leave the kitchen table. I went outside and literally sobbed.

The whole reentry process has been challenging, with lots of emotions attached. After a bad accident, your brain shuts down for a reason, protecting you in ways you may not completely understand, but that's okay. I think a lot of people instinctively sensed this and knew when I was ready to hear their part of the story.

Part of my recovery from a brain trauma injury was dealing with post-traumatic stress disorder or PTSD. Thank goodness a dear friend recommended I go see a therapist, which I never thought of doing until November of 2014, a year after the accident. Honestly, it is really important for anyone who goes through a life-changing experience to get help and guidance in dealing with this part of the healing process.

After our first session, my therapist told me I was grieving. I thought he meant that I was still grieving over the loss of my mom, dad, and Aviana, who had recently passed on. He looked right at me and said, "I mean you, personally." At that moment, it was like a light switch turned on in my brain. Yes, I was indeed grieving what I had lost, finding my place in life again and not knowing exactly how to move forward with the film projects. Realizing this shook me to the core of my being.

Dr. Connelly explained to me the list of steps one goes through in the grieving process. I checked off each one of them. I went on to tell him that I had left my professional career as a Visual Effects Producer in New York City and moved back to Nebraska to produce the film project I was so passionate about. I wanted to make it into a feature film. All of that seemed to have been stripped away, and now I was in an entirely different situation, trying to figure out who I was and how to get there. Everything was finally starting to click with more clarity and an understanding of why I had been feeling so emotional, and sometimes doubting my ability to do things the way I had done them before the accident. It was time to figure out what my new "normal," was and embrace it.

I also started meeting with Brother August, my spiritual director at Mt. Michael, to discuss where I was spiritually and my current relationship with God. I felt myself emerging from a place of solitude, like being in the desert. I had a quieter, calmer awareness of myself. This was the first time in my life I was actually at a place where I could be still and listen.

When my son came to see me in September of 2014, he asked me if I was afraid to die. I said no, and told him about my experience in the spirit world. Then he asked me if I wanted to go back there. I told him I had thought about it, but no. At this stage of my recovery, I was going through a difficult time emotionally, not knowing how to be a part of the film projects I started before my accident. Through this whole experience, I have never questioned my place in life. It is here on this earth taking the steps to move forward, embracing every part of it. There is a much more complex captivating world out there, and I got a glimpse of it. I will always hold that experience dear. What an amazing gift to have been blessed with.

My faith has been pivotal throughout my life and has grown immensely as I go through these changes. When your life suddenly stops, it is quite an unfamiliar feeling to grasp. Before the accident, I was constantly busy, pursuing my career and the new film project I had dreamed about doing for many years. I sensed God's presence protecting me, guiding me, and healing me in ways I had never known or been aware of before. You have to find your own way back, but you need the support of family, friends, and God's nurturing, protective guidance.

When I was at the hospital, scar tissue had formed where the tracheostomy tube was put in. It got more and more difficult to swallow food or liquid. The next time I saw the plastic surgeon, Dr. Bhuller, he looked at it. He had done surgeries to clean up scar tissue like that before. He did the surgery a couple of months later in September, 2015. Now I could swallow comfortably without any problems.

A month later, ready or not, I moved into my own apartment in Lincoln, walking distance to my friends Cathy and John's place. It was really great to be in a city where I had lived before with lots of friends around me to help me through this next big transition.

I started to go see films at the independent film theater, the Ross, on the University of Nebraska campus where I had often gone before when I was in high school. This had been a regular part of my life in my teens and during my profession as a film producer. One of the first films I saw was *Room*. Such a powerful well-done film. The story centers on the mother and little boy escaping their abductor. Once they escape, the story follows their reentry into the real world. The similarities were striking and touched me deeply.

Throughout my recovery, things like travel, physical conversations, reading by myself or out loud with a friend, playing a card game, watching a show, taking walks in a beautiful natural setting like the Sunken Gardens, hearing and watching birds, listening to music—all these kept me balanced, feeling grateful and so blessed to be alive.

Another story that really struck me was one my friend Cathy told me. She saw me earlier the day before they were going to unplug the equipment. She drove home to Lincoln and sat on her back patio with a glass of wine, trying to absorb the reality that she had just said goodbye to me. As she sat outside on their patio, she felt Crazy Horse's presence, letting her know that he did not want to be the center of attention in any way; the focus needs to be on his people, the Lakota. In other words, not to make a film about him as the central character.

My option for the Crazy Horse *script was up in the summer of 2015, and Timon did not want to extend it or give me credit for the year and a half I lost because of the accident, so I no longer had the film project. This was when Cathy told me this story.*

A big part of my recovery has been reengaging in all of life's complexities, no matter how difficult or challenging they may be. Writing this memoir has been part of my therapy, piecing together my life all the way up through the accident and recovery. I was back in my element; seeing more films in the theater was such a joy. The film *Arrival* was another one that deeply affected me. Every part of that film—the directing, acting, set design, scoring, editing—resonated with me. There are parts of the story that reflect things I experienced in the beginning of my recovery. The story line moved back and forth between linear time and nonlinear time with dramatic events in between that led to the conclusion of the surprising ending. It was astounding to watch this film unfold and reflect on the similarities to my own experience.

The first year, there were fleeting glimpses of a reality I recognized and remembered, but they were random. It was about two-and-a-half years later when I had a clear awareness of living a normal day-to-day life again. In the beginning of my recovery, it felt like I was going from a nonlinear to linear sense of existence.

When your life abruptly stops, coming back to the real world again is quite a process, and it does not happen in a straightforward way. The film project I had moved back to

Nebraska to work on went away, so I was also facing how to let go of that at the same time. Honestly, those projects spurred me on, pushing me to get back to work on them. Losing both projects was very humbling. It was time to rediscover myself and take the steps to embark on a new journey in the midst of my recovery. I am so blessed to have the support and encouragement from my wonderful son, family, and friends, as well as staying grounded in my faith.

Another situation I had problems with was facial recognition, which I recently found out is one of the effects from the brain trauma. I noticed this earlier but did not understand it was a problem until I heard a story on NPR discussing it with a clinical doctor. With more clarity, I understood why it was difficult to find someone in a large group of people. Now I always go with someone or pick a specific place to meet.

It is important to understand that when you are with someone going through recovery from a severe accident like brain trauma, you should keep conversations with them going, even though the person may not be participating. I do not remember all of the conversations going on around me when I was in the hospital or at the beginning of my stay at Madonna, but my gut sense is they sparked significant parts of my brain to start functioning again.

Having a purpose in life is essential. It was having a goal to focus on that helped me get through some of those big challenges with my health and a sense of well-being. This is something I had not struggled with for a long time, but it now seems to be more difficult at times as I go through this. It is easy to be consumed by it, questioning and being more acutely aware when something does not feel right physically. Then it starts affecting me on every level. That is when I go back to focusing on how to find answers, the right ones with the right doctor. This part of the process is quite challenging as well.

I had started planning a trip to New York and Europe to celebrate turning the big 60. My trip was set for the month of May in 2016, almost three years after my accident. I was very excited about taking this trip, visiting Julie and George in New York City, my dear friend Iris in Paris, and Nolan in Budapest. I had traveled to California and New York the year before, but a trip abroad to Europe would be the next big step in my recovery. I felt ready to reach a little further past my comfort zone. All of these thoughts were my focus during the two months before my trip, but I only made it to New York City. When I arrived at La Guardia, my double vision that had started a year ago in 2015 had gotten so acute I could not read the signs and had to ask where to go to get a cab into the city. This included the bright lighting, which was either double or blurred in the distance. Talk about being debilitated—I knew then it was a serious problem.

During my visit to New York City, my friend Julie told me that when they were about to unplug me from the ventilators, she and her husband George decided to wait for the call from my brother Mark at a spot in Central Park I had walked by with them many times before, reminiscing over stories when I frequently stayed with them. She had told me this story when I visited them the first time after the accident in April, 2015, but I had not remembered it this time.

When I visited Julie and George in February of 2020, I pointed out to them that this is stored in my memory with a clear awareness of the emotional significance of moments like this one.

In my gut, I knew it was not possible to travel to Europe until the double vision problem was figured out. I was not completely ready to accept this until I talked to my son about it. I explained to him how much worse it had gotten, and he advised me to wait. It was his wise advice that convinced me to go back home. Honestly, this was a good test run for me, having to deal with all the changes with my tickets, weather delays, and traveling late at night. I made it back to Omaha in the midst of a severe thunderstorm. We were the last plane to land before they closed the airport.

When I got home, the first step was an appointment with my internist, Dr. Shehan. He sent me in for an MRI and reviewed it with the doctor from Creighton, concerned I might have had a small stroke due to all the scar tissue I had in my brain. But the good news was that it looked the same as the one after the accident. Dr. Shehan gently reminded me that I will never be a typical patient after everything I have been through since my accident. This prompted me to finally accept my new "normal."

I had already gone to two eye doctors in Lincoln the year before to figure out this problem but they had both misdiagnosed what was going on. The next step was, Dr. Shehan sent me to a neuro-ophthalmologist, Dr. Legge. On my first visit, he properly diagnosed the problem: I had diplopia, which means my left eye was turning inward, causing the double vision. This was treatable by putting prisms on a pair of glasses adjusting my vision to the center, which seemed to solve the problem in the beginning.

When I was going through more of my files for the *Crazy Horse* film, I found paperwork and photos of the beautiful saddle blanket that my mother had grown up with. It was given to her as a gift when her dad taught at a school in Custer, South Dakota. So it had always been in our family and eventually had been passed on to me. Part of my plan before the accident was to use it in some of the horseback riding scenes in the film. Thank goodness all of the paperwork from the Gerald Ford Conservation Center was in one of the files. Then I remembered more details, how my cousin John had recommended I take it there to be evaluated to make sure it was in a good enough condition to use. So many things came flooding back to me.

Since I no longer had the option for the *Crazy Horse* script, I asked my brothers if we could donate the saddle blanket to a museum since it was made in the late 1800s with exquisite glass beads done by a Plains Indian tribe, most likely Lakota. With the help of my friend, Chuck, who is Lakota, the Heritage Center at Red Cloud Indian School in Pine Ridge accepted it. My friends Cathy and John kindly drove me up there to deliver the blanket. The last time I was in Pine Ridge was three months before the accident when I was producing the documentary for the *Crazy Horse Ride* in June of 2013.

I went ahead and rescheduled my trip to New York City and Europe for the month of October in 2016. It was my first trip internationally since the accident, and I had a fantastic time, but my double vision kept shifting when I was there. As soon as I got back, I went to see Dr. Legge, and he adjusted the prism, which helped, but my left eye kept moving inward. By the summer of 2017, my sixth cranial nerve had stopped functioning altogether. This time, Dr. Legge told me there was nothing more he could do at that time. This had an extremely debilitating effect on my ability to function. My balance was completely off. I could drive a little bit as long as I wore a patch over my left eye, but the double vision still limited my ability to drive. I was struggling emotionally to have come so far in my recovery, and then this really hit me hard.

I was perplexed why this problem was on the left side of my head, since the horse had landed on top of the right side. It did not make sense until I brought this up with Brother Mel. He pointed out that as the horse landed on me, the weight pushed the left side of my head further into the small chunks of gravel that were on that road. For the first time, it made sense. This is what caused the hole in my carotid artery and my eye problem, which were both on the left side.

In August of 2017, Matt, Angel's husband, who is a medical doctor, had been observing this development, called Dr. Thorell's office to explain my situation. Given my history, they got me in to see him the following week. Dr. Thorell was still a bit surprised to see me, this time with a different problem. His first response when he looked at me was how much my left eye had moved over toward my nose, not moving at all. He commented that "Your situation is like a locomotive train out of control." The last time he saw me was three years ago when he had diagnosed and fixed the carotid cavernous fistula. He did have a solution for this, explaining in detail a new device called a flow diverter (Pipeline Embolization Device, Medtronic, Inc.) that had been developed two years ago and was recently approved by the FDA. It was used to shrink aneurysms, which he strongly felt was the cause for the sixth cranial nerve to stop functioning.

During this conversation he told me I was the first patient of his to recover so successfully from a traumatic brain injury, plus I was the first patient of his with this problem. That comment by itself struck me emotionally. I felt overwhelmed by the gravity of the situation but also at how fortunate I was to be sitting in that room with Dr. Thorell as he laid out the next step that could solve it.

He highly recommended I go ahead with the procedure, but there was no guarantee it would completely solve the problem. Given Dr. Thorell's track record with me, the odds of this being successful were pretty high. He called me a few days later to walk me through the whole process a second time, giving me a very clear understanding of how this would go and having me agree to take one aspirin a day for the rest of my life, starting after the surgery. As he listened to my concerns, I explained to him that out of all the other problems I had faced since the accident, this one affected me the most, emotionally and physically. After our

On the beautiful Danube River, with my son Nolan in Budapest, Hungary, October of 2016. This was my first trip in Europe since the accident and I was so happy to be spending a week with him, exploring this fascinating city.

conversation, I called his physician assistant, Brandon, the next day to let him know I wanted to go ahead with the procedure.

An angiogram was scheduled for August 17, 2017. This was the second one I had done with Dr. Thorell. He knew the problem was located near the carotid artery on the left side of my head he repaired three years ago. But this time the problem was near my sixth cranial nerve. The challenge was to find the exact spot where to place the Pipeline flow diverter.

As they wheeled me into to the surgery room, this time I was sharply present and cognizant of what was going on. During the procedure, I had conversations with Dr. Thorell the whole time. This was possible because the anesthesiologist did not put me completely under. Once the camera was in, Dr. Thorell looked at the images in real time on a large screen, assessing what was going on in that area of my brain. When he was ready to take a photo, I had to lie there, perfectly still, holding my breath.

About halfway through, he told me to look over at the large screen, pointing to the strips of platinum threaded together, closing up the large hole in my main left artery he had repaired. It still was in place, which was a very good sign. Talk about a trippy but fascinating experience, I marveled at his incredible expertise as he meticulously maneuvered along my carotid artery and found the spot that confirmed I had a pseudoaneurism, which caused the six cranial nerve to stop functioning.

The pipeline embolization device procedure was done on November 8, 2017 and Dr. Thorell nailed it. The surgery was a complete success. It stopped the aneurysm from growing. The left eye began to be more flexible, moving back toward the center but not completely. The medial rectus muscle had gotten stretched out, but was not fully functioning yet. A year later, Dr. Legge told me that muscle was not going to improve and recommended muscle surgery for the left eye. This involved a Hummelsheim transposition procedure along with medial rectus recession in that eye. This was the only alternative available to get my left eye to be positioned in the center. This procedure would keep the eye in place, allowing some up and done movement. In December of 2018, I had that surgery done, and it was successful. I will be forever grateful to both Dr. Thorell and Dr. Legge. For the first time since the accident, I am ready to move forward with my life!

After completing this chapter, I had no intention of writing more because this was challenging enough, but my therapist suggested I continue to write, starting at the beginning of my life. Little did I realize at the time she suggested this that it would unlock more memories, further accelerating my recovery. The rest of the chapters in this book are written in chronological order.

2

Discovering the Map:
The Early Days

As I began this chapter, three years after the accident, during the summer of 2016, more memories consistently flooded into my conscious mind. I started to jot down an outline, using it as a guide, to flesh out moments in my life that were pivotal to write about. Throughout the rest of the book, you will see how my thought process and vocabulary steadily improves, revealing a clearer picture of "me."

Growing up in a small town in the late 1950s was a unique experience for me. We lived in Osmond, Nebraska, population of 750 people. A lot of my relatives on the Theisen side lived in town and out on the farms. When I was about three or four years old, I would pick up the phone and ask the voice on the other end, "Could I please talk to my grandma?" Magically, my grandma's voice appeared on the other end. The operators in town must have had a chuckle when they picked up the call, knowing who was calling from the phone number. This was small town life in 1958 and 1959 in northeast Nebraska.

We lived on the edge of town with a large yard, garden,

treehouse in the willow tree, and a pasture near a creek. The Catholic school I went to was up the street right next to the church where we attended mass. I often walked over to my grandma's house a couple blocks from us. If it was breakfast time, she would make my favorite pancakes with a cup of coffee made with a lot of milk. Usually on Sundays we had dinner at Grandma and Grandpa's house. After dinner, no one was allowed to clean up right away. We would always visit and sometimes watch *Walt Disney's Wonderful World of Color* splashing across the television. My mom and grandma were excellent cooks, so we always had delicious homemade meals and desserts made from our gardens during the summer and beef or lamb from relatives who raised them on their farms outside of town.

When I was five years old, Grandpa Theisen bought two Shetland ponies for us. There are photos of my sister, brothers, and me riding Sally, the mare. In one photo I have a big smile on my face. I was the youngest and from the beginning, showed a keen interest in the ponies. Sally had two colts: the first one, Decidedly, was named after the 1962 Kentucky Derby winner, and the second colt was Chateaugay, the 1963 winner. Taking care of those ponies and riding were two of my favorite things to do growing up.

One of the pastures where we kept the ponies was next to the football field where the Osmond High School Tigers played their home games. On one of those nights, it was particularly cold. A lot of people sat in their cars, including my parents, to stay warm and watch the game. I could hear the ponies whinnying from the car, so I decided to go over to find out what was going on, not telling my parents where I was going. I thought they needed to be calmed down from all the crowd noise. Decidedly was running up and down when I slid under the fence into the pasture. She raced past me, bucked up her hind legs, and hit me squarely in the chin. It stung, and I knew something was seriously wrong. I walked back to the car where Mom and Dad were and knocked on the car window. I was wearing a pair of white gloves that had turned bright red. My mom looked at me, smiling, then her face turned completely ashen.

The town's local doctor, Dr. Mallard, was at the football game, too. We found him and went to his office in the basement of his house. It was such a shock for my mom to see this big cut on my chin, so my sister Diane stayed with me and held my hand as the doctor stitched up the cut. The whole time I was very quiet, and later on I explained to my parents that it was not Decidedly's fault. The loud noise from the crowd was what scared her. I was trying my best to make sure I could still be around the ponies and go horseback riding. After all these years, the scar on my chin is still visible, along with my memory of how it happened.

When my dad served in the navy during WWII, he was stationed at the Brooklyn Navy Yard in New York City. He told stories about going into Manhattan to hear live jazz for the first time. This was around 1945. Some of the records I heard growing up were Dave Brubeck, Stan Getz, and Herb Alpert & the Tijuana Brass. My mom and dad played them on our RCA Victor stereo console. This rich, sophisticated, complex style of music is what developed my lifelong interest and love for jazz.

I was probably about eight years old when I had my appendix taken out. During the time I was in the hospital, Mom told me the ponies whinnied every day. My brother John was put in charge of taking care of them until I got back. It took several weeks before I was allowed to see the ponies and pet them outside the fence. They were happy to see me and finally stopped whinnying.

During high school I worked summers for my dad's heavy highway construction company, Theisen Brothers, and so did my brothers. Grandpa Theisen started this company in the early 1920s, keeping him and several of his brothers employed. Dad grew up in the business and eventually took it over for many years until he retired.

My childhood was filled with family, cousins, and the ponies. In the summer of 1971, we moved to Lincoln, Nebraska, to begin my sophomore year at Pius X high school. My quarter horse, Lady Chestnut, moved with us. We had lived in Lincoln three years earlier when my Mom went back to college to get her degree in interior design at the University of Nebraska. I was excited to be back in Lincoln, but I dearly missed my relatives and friends in Osmond and Norfolk.

We moved into a house my mom designed on the north shore of Capital Beach Lake, close to downtown Lincoln. The design was an open plan with high ceilings and light streaming in through large windows, with panoramic views of the city. The house was built out of brick, all of which were from jobs Theisen Brothers had done in small towns around the state, mostly Wayne, Nebraska. All of us had helped clean up the bricks for the house on the lake. The view at night with the lights glistening off the lake was stunning. We had a sailboat docked right next to the house. My brother Mark and Mom really enjoyed sailing, so I often went out with them to crew. My years living there were wonderful. Often we had a full house, with my brother John living there when he attended college at UNL and Grandad living with us for a year before he moved back to Northern California.

My sister Diane and I were always very close. The story my Dad told me was she had prayed for a baby sister, and it had been answered when I arrived home. She and I were eight years apart, and she always looked out for me, which she continues to do each day. Diane was very involved in politics, starting in high school with the Catholic Youth Organization (CYO). It was her passion. During college, she was the president of ASUN Student Government at the University of Nebraska for a couple of years. When they were getting ready for the march on the state capitol steps to protest against the Vietnam War and Cambodian invasion, I helped make armbands with the peace sign for protesters to wear around their arms. So many things happened during those formative years for me in Lincoln during high school.

The pasture where my horse was stabled was on the other side of town, close to Holmes Lake. The area, known as horse country in the 1970s, is now filled with houses. There were a lot of other horse people who either lived or stabled their horses in the area. My parents drove me out often, which was about a half-hour trip each way. I always looked forward to going out there, taking long rides down those country roads. There was a riding stable nearby where I took English riding lessons. I thoroughly enjoyed this style of riding. As my skills improved, I began to compete in three-day equestrian events. I loved every part of it. The feeling I had when I was flying up over those tall wide jumps was exhilarating, like floating through air, being one with the horse.

The first year in Lincoln, I was focused on riding and high school. This pleasant routine was going to change. The drama teacher at my high school was planning a trip to Europe for four weeks the following summer. She taught drama, my favorite class, and was also one of my favorite teachers. The thought of traveling abroad intrigued me. When I took the information home to show my parents, I think they saw it as an opportunity for me to experience new places and cultures. They told me I could go and would pay for half of the trip, but I had to come up with the money for the other half. The only way I could do this was to sell my horse. Much later, I realized, it was their way of helping me move past that part of my life. This was the most difficult decision to make, but I knew deep down it was going to change my life. I just did not know how yet.

A ranch family from the western part of Nebraska bought my horse. When I said goodbye to my beautiful quarter horse, Lady Chestnut, I cried. The commitment to start the next chapter of my life had begun. My parents knew if I was away from home for a month, it would help me get over not having my horse. Mom and Dad had made a wise choice, helping me embark on a new adventure.

At the same time, my interest in film continued to grow. When I was nine years old, my parents took me to see *Cat Ballou* at the theater in Osmond. It was a Western comedy made in 1965 with Lee Marvin and Jane Fonda in the lead roles. I remember being enthralled by this movie. I asked my parents to see it again. Six years later, we moved to Lincoln, Nebraska, and started going to see foreign and independent films at the Sheldon Art Museum on the University of Nebraska campus.

The films I saw there captivated my curiosity on so many levels. They awakened something in me, an awareness of a much larger, complex world out there that I had no idea existed. The stories resonated across socioeconomic and cultural spheres in how they were interpreted or perceived. They were glimpses into other people's lives and the worlds they lived in. What and how these films were made is something I knew I wanted to be a part of early on.

It was the early 1970s when I was watching these films at Sheldon from a lot of different directors. Some of my favorites are Lina Wertmuller, Federico Fellini, Jean-Luc Goddard, John Cassavetes, Vittorio De Sica, John Sayles, Jim Jarmusch, Akira Kurosawa, and Robert Altman, to name a few. Two films that impacted me then were *Walkabout*, directed by Nicolas Roeg, and *Ramparts of Clay*, directed by Jean-Louis Bertucelli. The first film was about two young British siblings who experience a tragic situation and get lost in the Australian outback. They are befriended by an indigenous man who guides them back to civilization. The striking contrast between these two very different worlds was visually and dramatically played out in the story. The second film was a story about a remote village in the northern part of Africa. The villagers face the encroachment of modern civilization as it threatened their simple primitive lives. They struggled to keep their way of life going. There was very little dialogue spoken as the story unfolded through the visual beauty and purity as they held on to their way of life.

All of these films gave me a visual picture of different cultures, languages, topography, architecture, and foods that offered a variety so completely foreign from what I knew growing up in Nebraska. Watching these subtle nuances unfold created a desire in me to explore more. To this day, a well-done film sparks a gut response, the combination of the visual, the characters—everything. If the film draws me in, it just really impacts me. It makes me think about more things or different ways of looking at things, not forming an opinion, but understanding them, being more curious and wanting to know more. I was always intrigued about the process, thinking through why the director and editor choose a particular shot and how they cut shots together in the scene. And why did they shoot at that angle or why did they light the scene in a certain way? What I realized early on is that the whole process of making a film is very complex—the location, lighting, acting, sound, music, the script, and character develop throughout the story. It just really blew me away, understanding how complex it is to get all of that up there on the screen. It's not easy. This art form was beginning to draw me in.

Those films were part of my education and widened my sense of how richly diverse this world is. They also taught me how to observe the scope and vastness of the earth we live on. This is what I recognized and absorbed from a complex story as it played out in front of me on that big screen. I still prefer watching a film in the theater, no distractions with your devices, just being completely present, drawn in to what is going on within the film. They are meant to be experienced visually on a big screen. The experience you have in a theater is not the same as seeing it on a small screen.

Watching those films is what spurred my curiosity during my teenage years; preparing me to go out there and explore more of the world. The summer of 1972 is when I went with a group of students from my high school to Europe. Looking back on it now, Sister Francis was a brave soul to take a group of fifteen-to-seventeen-year-old students on their first trip abroad, away from home.

The trip began in Ireland. After we got over the jet lag, we went to Bunratty Castle, near Limerick. The countryside was filled with deep, rich green hues. When we arrived at the castle, they gave us a welcome reception with an amazing medieval banquet. All of this made me feel like I was in my element; it sparked my curiosity to be in this new environment.

The next day, we traveled south along the stunning Atlantic Ocean and the Ring of Kerry to the city of Killarney. The Irish brogue was lovely. Sometimes I heard a different accent, which I thought was a foreign language, but we were still in Ireland. I soon learned it was Gaelic and could not understand a word of it.

My best friend, Cathy, was my roommate during the trip. We had a routine. After dinner we went out to sightsee on our own. One of the stops was the local pub. It was a lively atmosphere filled with lots of laughter and singing. This is where I had my first glass of Guinness.

Our next stop was Blarney Castle. The place is legendary for many reasons, especially to kiss the Blarney stone. We all climbed up the steep steps to a narrow part in the wall where you have to lie down on your back, slide underneath it, and kiss the stone, with the hope you would receive the gift of eloquence. There are legends told about well-known writers and poets who have kissed it, too.

When we arrived on the main land, one of the things I discovered was a different kind of chocolate, particularly dark chocolate. Each time the bus stopped for gas, I went into the store to check out the wide array of big chunks of chocolate in round containers. None of it was packaged like the candy bars at home. The entire trip broadened my education in new ways. As we traveled to other countries in Europe, I discovered the mini-bar in the hotel room. I quickly learned that whatever was in there was not free.

I still vividly remember many of the experiences on this trip. During our visit to Rome, we attended an open-air opera sung in Italian with no subtitles. This, my first time seeing opera live, was amazing. Even though I did not understand the words, as the story unfolded, the music, opera singers, set design, and the costumes drew me into the story. Rome was and still is one of my favorite cities. To walk around the old cobblestone streets and peek into a beautiful old courtyard in the old part of the city was magical. There were sounds of the church bells ringing at certain times of the day. The colors of the older buildings had a soft warm patina. The city was filled with a vital rich history that was still very much alive. It felt inviting with a pace that was not rushed.

We toured the Vatican and some of the churches in the old part of Rome. There were magnificent frescos and paintings in each place and often the fragrance of incense. When I sat in the Sistine Chapel and looked up at the stunning painted frescoes, I felt a sense of awe and reverence. All of the churches we visited had candles you could light and offer up a prayer. This was something I did with Grandma Theisen early in my childhood when we lived in Osmond. I did this at each church we visited throughout the trip—lighting a candle and saying a prayer for my family and loved ones just as she had done.

In the old part of Rome where our hotel was located, there were pieces of art or sculpture in every direction, always in a public space for everyone to see. A lot of the sculptures, architecture, and paintings in Rome are by the Italian baroque artist Gian Lorenzo Bernini, done in 1621 to 1625. Our last night in Rome we went to one of the biggest tourist sites in the city. As we walked down a cobblestone street, we could hear the sound of water. As we turned the corner, there was the spectacular Trevi Fountain, all lit up. I threw a coin in with my right hand over my left shoulder to ensure I would return to Rome. This is one of my rituals when ever I visit Rome. So far, it has worked.

The fragrance in each city we visited was often so different from anything I had known before. As I walked down the streets in these cities, there were so many kinds of foods I smelled that often led me to a street vendor or inside a food shop. In Italy there were different kinds of pizza and gelato that were not like the Valentino's pizza I ate at home in Lincoln. I am pretty sure it was in Italy when I started to notice my pants had gotten uncomfortably tight. My experiences on this trip widened my awareness and appreciation for lots of new things that included food.

This also brought back fond memories of the summer vacations I took with my family when I was growing up, exploring different parts of the U.S. and Canada in our station wagon. Sometimes my sister and I would put on little dramas when it was our turn to sit in the rear seat, keeping us entertained, along with the people who drove past us. This time, traveling outside the U.S. was an entirely different experience. Midway through our tour, I was keenly aware that I belonged in Europe.

Paris—ah, Paris. For whatever reason, this was the place for me. The day we arrived, I felt a strong connection to the city. We had toured through Europe for three weeks, and this was the last week of our trip. The people, their sense of style, the language, the food—all seemed to click with me more than any of the other places we visited. On our last day in Paris, Cathy and I explored more of the city on our own. We ended up in the middle of a large student protest. By the time we found our way back to the hotel, it was late. We missed dinner and the city of lights tour at night. There were plenty of reasons for me to return to Paris.

Our last three days on the trip were in London. It was nice to be back in an English-speaking country after three-and-a- half weeks of several other languages. The last night, Cathy and I went out and ended up at Piccadilly Circus. At this time it was a large enough square for people to congregate. There we met two guys from Killarney, Ireland, John and Gerry. Amazingly, it was one of our first stops on the tour that we had really enjoyed. We exchanged addresses and went back to the hotel.

It was that night in London my friend Cathy met her future husband, John. They have been happily married for many years, living in the states and frequently going back to visit family in Ireland. Often, I ask them to tell their sweet story about how they met on the last day of our trip.

When we waited to board the plane at Heathrow Airport, a big part of me wanted to stay in Europe. I did not know how to accomplish this yet, but I knew I would figure out a way to return soon. After we got back to Lincoln, a month later, we started our junior year at Pius X High School. As first semester began, a group of us began to discuss ways to graduate early. The school had changed to the modular system the previous year that allowed students to fit in more classes to complete the requirements needed to graduate in a year. After we figured which classes, seven of us signed up and completed them our junior year. By the time the principal found out what we had done, it was too late to change it. The seven of us, all women that included Cathy and me, graduated a year early, skipping our senior year. We graduated with the senior class of 1973 even though they were not happy about it. Right after we did that, the school changed the rules so it was no longer possible to graduate a year early.

After I graduated from high school, I wanted to return to Europe and study film. I decided on Paris. During the summer I worked for Theisen Brothers to earn enough money for the trip. Even though I was only seventeen years old, amazingly my parents let me go. In the fall of 1973, I left Lincoln and moved to Paris, the City of Lights. I got a job as an au pair with a family that had three very active young boys. I watched them in the mornings and evenings, with one day off during the week. The mother was from the U.S., and the father was from Brazil, so the boys mostly spoke French and Portuguese. Their mother wanted me to speak American English in the home around the boys, so it all worked out well.

I knew a little bit of French from the classes I took in high school, but the Parisian accent is quite different from what I had learned. After I started my au pair job, I was eager to learn more French. I signed up for a beginner's French class at the Sorbonne. Out of the entire class, three of us were from the United States; everyone else was from other parts of the world. Only French was spoken during class. The structure started out with simple words, rapidly building up a French vocabulary. This style of teaching worked well for me. A couple of weeks into the class, the teacher said something to the three of us in perfect English, complimenting us on how quickly we were picking up the language. This cracked me up because it had not occurred to me she had understood everything we had discussed in English during class.

Two dear friends of the family I had known since grade school lived in Paris. Iris and Burt were immensely helpful as I got situated in my new surroundings. They were my second parents. We often met for coffee or dinner at their place when I had the day off. Those first couple of months were so enjoyable. They took me to see films at the Cinémathèque Française located at the Palais de Chaillot on the Right Bank, near where I lived. There, an incredible array of films by independent directors was shown—I was back in my element. I had not done a lot of research regarding film programs, but I knew there were several schools and universities in Paris, including the American University. I soon found out the only way to study film was through a graduate program.

This certainly narrowed my options to attend film school. The only way to study film was to return to the States. I left Paris around Christmas in 1973 and returned to Lincoln. The spring of 1974, I got accepted into an experimental program called Centennial College at the University of Nebraska. They did not have a film program yet, but students lived on campus and attended their classes in the same place as a community. Individually, you created your own curriculum similar to an independent study. Professors helped me put together one that focused on watching, analyzing, and critiquing films, film theory, script writing, and photography. Throughout the semester, I was evaluated by the professor and graded. It was a perfect way for me to begin learning about film. During that year, I applied to schools on the east coast and got accepted into the film program at Syracuse University in upstate New York. I spent the next three years fully immersed in studying, writing, producing, crewing and my senior film thesis.

3

Adventures in Alaska

After I graduated from college with a degree in film, I realized finding a job in the film industry was going to be pretty difficult. I don't think my heart was in it anyway. So when a friend of mine from high school asked me if I wanted to go to Alaska with her to commercial fish, it sounded like quite an adventure, so I said yes. I started saving my money and made plans for my big trip to Alaska. The state was trying to dissuade people from coming up. You had to have at least $1,000 if you were moving there. This was May 1980.

I headed to Idaho the end of April to pick up my friend Jenny. When I got to her house, she had decided not to go. I was going, period. When my sister Diane found out I was going on my own, she enlisted a friend, Steve Potter, to chaperone me. Steve's a lawyer and was the district attorney in Grand Island, Nebraska. He was a great traveling partner. We met at the ferry terminal in Seattle, Washington, where the Alaska Marine Ferries docked. We bought groceries for the trip and staked out our chaise lounge chairs on the top deck of the ferry. The deck was walled in with clear plexiglass that formed a U shape to keep you protected from the elements. It was completely open, looking out over the stern of the ship. We had the best view on the entire boat. No privacy, but that didn't matter. Most of us were in our early twenties, headed up for a new adventure. Almost everyone was returning to Alaska to either fish or work in the canneries in Southeast Alaska. After we got settled, I explored the rest of the boat. It was almost comical to see so many people reading John McPhee's book *Coming into the Country* about his recent travels in Alaska. Several people were talking about their own experiences fishing in Alaska. It was a whole new world to me, literally.

Potter and I decided to take the ferry all the way to Sitka, the last stop. This would take a little over three days traveling through the Inside Passage. It was spectacular, brimming with rich wildlife and fauna, quite exotic to a Nebraska girl. There were white spots in the trees that I discovered were eagles. Orca fins would quietly appear, gliding through the dark water alongside the ferry. As we passed tiny islands, I saw rustic cabins tucked into inlets. I wondered who lived there and how they survived the wilds of Alaska. I would soon find out.

One of my routines during the trip was to go to the bar in the evening and see who was hanging out. There were usually a few people from the solarium, so I would join them. This particular time several people were sitting around a woman with golden blond hair and brilliant sky blue eyes. Everyone was completely captivated listening to her story. Her name was Nance. She had gone out to crew on a fishing boat with the skipper, Rick, the previous year in early November, the end of the Dungeness crab season. They were pulling up pots when a heavy storm blew in. The waves crashed relentlessly over the boat. The boat started to take on water. Rick knew they were sinking. I sat there in stunned silence listening and wondering what the hell I was getting myself into. He put Nance in the one and only survival suit on board the boat. I had no idea what a survival suit was or why I would need one. He put her in the suit and zipped it up just as the boat went under. They were both in the cold, icy ocean in the pitch dark while the storm raged on. All he had on were the clothes he had been fishing in. Nance held on to him tightly. He started to go limp from the hypothermia. She struggled to hold on but couldn't any longer. When she let go, the ocean suddenly became calm for a brief moment. The reality that he had just died overwhelmed her. The waves crashed over her, snapping her into the realization that if she didn't start swimming she was going to die, too. Swimming in the oversized survival suit was very awkward. The only open area was around her face. She had no idea which direction to go, but made up her mind to just start swimming. Miraculously she swam straight toward the shore.

Stranded on a pristine shoreline along Icy Strait in November was still perilous, to say the least. Planes and larger boats went by, but no one saw her. A few bright pink buoys from the boat floated to the shore. She dragged those with her as she walked up and down the beach hoping this would make it easier for the rescuers to spot her. There were brown bears around, but they were disinterested in her. She ate small green plants along a creek. The bright orange survival suit was the only thing that kept her warm. After eleven days of surviving on very little and walking the beach each day, one of the guys in the Coast Guard chopper spotted her. It was the last day of the rescue search for her. They immediately flew her to a hospital in Juneau to get checked out. From this whole experience, she had a little bit of frostbite on a couple of toes, but other than that she was okay, though much thinner and exhausted. Her story was reported in the news all over the United States, Canada, and Japan. I sat there even more stunned. I told her how much I admired her courage and will to survive through such adversity. Our friendship began that day. All of these years later, she is still one of my dearest friends.

I met a guy on the ferry, Mitch, who invited me to stay on an island in Sitka Sound where he was house sitting with his friends. The only way to get there was by boat. When we arrived in town, they were waiting for him at the dock just down from the infamous Pioneer Bar, the fishermen's bar. Off we went in this little black and white motorboat to the island. The house was very rustic with this amazing view of Mt. Edgecombe, an extinct volcano that looks a lot like Mt. Kilimanjaro. It was absolutely stunning with its white-capped rim. I ended up staying in the surf house on the other side of the island, a short walk from the main house. This little bungalow was at the top of a cliff where the waves crashed against the rocks below. The friends staying at the house were so welcoming and fun to hang out with. We had these great dinner parties. Afterwards, we went out in the row boat or took a walk around the island late at night when it was still light out. I loved it.

I went into town to look for work, what locals call "hitting the docks." Potter and I made quite a pair. It was pretty hilarious. Here's Potter walking down the ramp to the main fishing harbor with his jeans on, which is fine, but he also had his cowboy boots on. That was sort of a dead giveaway; obviously he had never fished before, nor had he ever come close to it. And then there's me, a woman with no experience either. I was surprised and encouraged to see several women crewing and running their own fishing boats out of Sitka. We both got a job on separate boats after a week of looking. My first boat was with this old guy in his seventies who had fished all his life. We went south into this beautiful fjord and fished for coho salmon. I had my first freshly caught salmon perfectly seared that night for dinner.

We anchored in front of Goddard Hot Springs. The setting was stunning. There were three large round wooden tubs filled with steaming hot water from the springs. They had a roof over them facing west so you have this incredible view of the sun setting over the ocean. Of course this doesn't happen until about 11P.M. There's also a house nearby where people can stay when it's available. The skipper told me I could take the skiff and row over to the shore. It had been a long day of fishing, pulling in the gear and cleaning fish, so I decided a good soak would help my sore, weary muscles. Well, it was quite a hilarious adventure. I had never rowed before. It was challenging, to say the least, and I kept going around in circles. Finally, I figured out how to go directly to the shore, but the guys in the hot tub cracked up the whole time.

When I finished the trip with the Skipper, I made enough money to stay on the island a little longer. Mitch was going up to Skagway to hike the Chilkat Trail. Since I had not found another job yet, I decided to go with him. We took the ferry north up to Skagway and started our hike from town. It follows the gold rush trail the miners took in the late 1800s up to the Yukon, near Dawson City. The trail was well marked with cabins along the way. It was pretty amazing to see rusted-out ironwood stoves, old bridle bits, and other odds and ends along the trail. The hike is gradual until you reach the scales that take you up to the top of the summit. We lucked out and had sunny weather the whole way up. Two days earlier they had a blizzard at the summit in the middle of June! The lakes up there are a deep emerald green and freezing cold.

On the hike down, we crossed over into Canada. There's a town—well, sort of—called Carcross. A train stops there once a week with supplies. We had our first cooked meal there after several days of eating freeze-dried food on our hike. From there we took the train to Whitehorse, where I stayed one night and then headed up to Dawson City for the summer solstice. The whole town was filled with tourists from all over the world to celebrate the event. A group of us from the hostel I stayed at joined hundreds of people on a mountain called the Dome to watch the sun rotate around it and dip slightly. On this day, June 21, in this part of the northern hemisphere, the sun does not set. Some famous writers lived there for a short period of time. The summer repertory theater performed live poetry readings on the porch of Robert Service's historically restored cabin in the center of town. In September of 1897, Jack London was twenty-one years old when he lived in Dawson City for a year to prospect for gold. He did not strike it rich, but from those experiences, he wrote, *The Call of the Wild.* I thoroughly enjoyed my visit there and learned a lot about the history of the Yukon.

From Dawson City I got a ride over the border into Alaska. We drove past Mt. McKinley and Denali and headed south to Anchorage. This took several days. Alaska is vast in size, especially when you drive through this part of the state. Anchorage was one wild city. I felt like I had been transported back into the Wild West. A lot of people I met worked on the pipeline and were in town for their week off. They told me there were plenty of jobs available up north on the pipeline. It sounded interesting, but I preferred the low-key craziness of Southeast Alaska. It was time for me to return to Sitka.

When I got back, I stayed at the surf house on the island. Having traveled to other parts of Alaska, I realized how special Sitka was. It was different from any other place I had lived. It felt magical to me. When I went into town to look for work, sometimes I took walks in Totem Park. It goes along the water's edge where you can look out at the islands in Sitka Sound. For me, this was a special place.

Certain times of the year, salmon go up the Indian River to spawn. The park was filled with large totem poles carved out of wood, some of which were very old and made by the Tlingit people, one of the indigenous tribes of Southeast Alaska. They tell stories about their history and culture. One of the legends was about the Kushtaka, the shape shifters in animal or human form, who usually come out at night and play tricks on you. A couple of times on my walks, I thought I saw them dart around one of the totem poles, although I was not exactly sure.

What I quickly ascertained about commercial fishing was that rarely did you discuss how dangerous this line of work was on a daily basis. Instead, everyone I knew embraced it. One of the things I learned my first season was the banter and dry humor that goes on pretty much all the time. A couple of people told me, in all seriousness, that the year before, Mt. Edgecombe was about to erupt, which would have devastated Sitka and the entire island, including all of the fishing fleet. This must have been a major story, so I asked some other fishermen about it. They just shrugged their shoulders. Finally, a friend told me a couple of fishermen had rented a plane, flown over Mt. Edgecombe and dropped some flaming tires that spewed smoke, making it look like it was about to blow. The locals knew it was a prank from the beginning. I heard plenty of similar hilarious stories when I lived there.

The coho salmon and black cod fishing seasons were in full swing after I got back. Most of the fishing boats already had their crews. The canneries and cold storage facilities were paying fishermen top dollar for their fish, putting everyone in a good mood. I was in the Pioneer Bar talking to some friends when I saw Nance. I was so happy to see her. She had not found work in Petersburg and decided to check out Sitka. A friend told her about a guy who had a live-aboard boat and was looking for someone to stay on it while he was out of town for work. The next day we met Wayne on his boat docked in the main harbor. It was an elegant Stephens yacht built in the 1940s, all teak, called the *Orca*. After we met, he hired both of us on the spot to live aboard his boat.

The accommodations were pretty deluxe with eight bunks and a nice sized, well-equipped galley with a stove, refrigerator, table, and washer/dryer. There was a large spacious deck the length of the boat. Now we had an amazing place to live! He gave us a list of jobs to do on the boat. We oiled every inch of the deck and polished all the brass those first couple of weeks. Wayne was gone most of the summer on surveying jobs located throughout Southeast Alaska. There was always lots of activity around us with commercial fishing boats coming and going, unloading their catch and gearing up for the next trip.

After a month on the *Orca*, Smitty, a fisherman and poet laureate, offered to take us to Godard Hot Springs on his boat, the *C Minor*. We took off on a warm sunny day, but the ocean got a bit rough on the way down. I started to get seasick, so I stayed on the back deck, trying to keep it together. Nance put on one of Smitty's survival suits and danced around on the back deck. It completely cracked me up. Somehow, my seasickness vanished.

We stayed in the main house the first night. It was so nice to soak in those hot tubs again as the sun set over the deep blue Pacific Ocean. I assumed, since we were in a remote part of Baranof Island, we would have a quiet evening, but no; two fishing boats anchored up, and the entire crew came in to soak. We hung out with them for a little bit and heard about some of their recent fishing escapades.

The next day we hiked up along the coast and spent the night in a very small Quonset hut by a lake. It was very rustic, as in no running water or toilet. In midsummer it gets slightly dark for a few hours, so I didn't sleep much. When I got up the next morning I was covered with little bites. So was Nance, but I definitely had more. That was my first introduction to these little tiny insects called no see-um's. Those bites itched for days. We cut our stay short and headed back to the hot springs.

This was the first of many adventures I would have with Nance. We hiked for about an hour, and it all seemed to look familiar. We had circled around the lake twice and but didn't realize it at first. The area had a lot of muskeg, which is a swamp or bog filled with a mixture of water and vegetation that is soft and spongy. If you step into one, you can fall a long ways down, because they are often deep and difficult to climb out of. We made a decision to go one direction away from the lake, but discovered an hour later it was the opposite way to the hot springs. I think at this point we decided to spend one more night in the hut. The next morning, we started out early and found the coastline. This time it led us back to the hot springs.

After we got back to town from our little adventure, I met Don, a skipper on the fishing boat called the *Charbus*. It was a beautiful older wood boat. Fishermen referred to it as skookum, which meant it had clean elegant lines and moved smoothly, balanced on the ocean, especially in rough seas.

He hired me the next day to fish the rest of the salmon season with him. His boat was a power troller, so commercial fishing is only permitted six miles or more off shore. There was a freezer set on the deck, so when the salmon had been cleaned, it was flash frozen there and put down in the hold. This method increased the value of the salmon, giving him a nice price when he sold them at the cold storage in Sitka.

It was midway through the salmon season, so we fished for all five species of salmon. Each kind used two names. The money fish was king (chinook), coho (silver), sockeye (red), pink (humpy), and chum (dog). I quickly learned how to tell them apart. The color, shape, and size were distinctly different. I learned different methods of how to prepare them, seared on an open fire on the beach, pan fried, smoked, and canned. All Alaskan salmon was absolutely delicious.

The knowledge required to successfully catch the illusive salmon was learned over years of fishing experience. When I started to crew on boats and watched how experienced fishermen worked, I noticed there was a great deal of experience required to be successful. They also had an acute awareness and sense of the ocean environment with constant weather changes.

Each fisherman I worked with had their own approach on how to find the fish and get them to bite. Sometimes it depended on the sound or shape of the boat as it moved through the water. This could either attract or chase the fish away. The type of gear was important, too, from the shape and color of a lure to the type of bait used on the hooks and how deep in the water to put the gear.

Don was a hi-liner, which meant he often caught a lot of fish each season. His boat had a freezer system onboard, so we stayed out and fished until the hold was full of salmon or we ran out of food. It was never the latter. Each trip we took was usually about three weeks long. I crewed for Don through the end of the salmon season my first year in Alaska.

Needless to say, when you crew on a commercial fishing boat, the skipper decides when to leave and how long to stay out on the fishing grounds. Another important aspect of commercial fishing was the right gear to wear. For me it was the Helly Hansen and Grunden rain gear and a pair of Xtratuf boots with wool socks. They kept you warm and dry in all kinds of weather conditions for the duration of the trip.

Another important piece of knowledge: skippers never left the dock on Friday the 13th. Several times we left for the fishing grounds exactly one minute after midnight, on the 14th. To add to this list of things not to do on a boat: above the sink in the galley is a place to hang coffee mugs. They always had to face in. When you're on the deck, never let the hatch cover land upside down. These were some of the things I learned my first season commercial fishing.

As summer rolled into fall, the northern lights danced across the night sky. I was in awe of this incredible light show. It did not matter where you were, inland or out on the ocean, flashes of brilliance just appeared, playing out a performance in the night sky. It was unlike anything I had ever experienced before.

There was a lot of terminology used on a commercial fishing boat I had to learn. When the skipper says the port side, you need to know it is the left side, starboard is the right side, front is the bow, and rear is the stern. I had no knowledge of these terms until I got my first job. Once you were out on the fishing grounds, usually several other fishing boats were out there, too, right alongside you.

The etiquette boats followed when it is crowded like that is, most importantly, to stay a certain distance apart to avoid collisions. But one trip, this is exactly what happened. Another boat got too close to the *Charbus* and cracked part of the middle outrigger or trolling pole. Since the town of Sitka was a couple hours away, Don decided to shimmy up the pole to repair it. It seemed simple enough until the waves increased in size and caused the boat to roll further from the port to the starboard side. With each wave, he dipped deeper into the water, then back up. What a harrowing experience to watch. Somehow he was able to jerry-rig the pole together so we could fish for a couple more days. When we got back to town, he had it welded together.

This was before cell phones, so the way I communicated with my friends when I got back to town was to write a note on the chalkboard at the office, aka The Pioneer Bar. It was always a hoot to see a note there to let me know if they were in town or out fishing. There were a few other bars in town, but this was known as the fishermen's bar, located right across the street from the main harbor in Sitka. This was the place to meet up, hang out, and hear live music. I had some of the most delicious smoked king salmon. Sometimes they had white king, which is more delicate with a richer flavor and texture. What a rare treat!

There were plenty of amusing things that happened on the fishing grounds. To call someone when you were out there, you had go through the marine operator on the radio. This meant everyone in the vicinity often listened to the conversation. This provided hours of entertainment. Believe me, I only used the radio for emergencies, but it was the best way for fishermen to keep in touch with their wives and families. We all knew more than you really wanted to know about those who were fishing around you. Sometimes it was like listening to a live soap opera.

Toward the end of the fishing season, Don decided to go up north to the Fairweather Grounds due west of Lituya Bay. The old timers all knew about these grounds. They were legendary. At least fifty miles off shore is this small shallow area that attracts large schools of nice sized king salmon, the money fish. We were in radio contact with Don's fishing buddies on the way up, hearing about their tallies of king salmon, but no one had found a big "bite" yet. When you're talking on the radio, everything is in code, but eventually you figure it out, especially when someone has found the fish, they usually can't conceal the excitement in their voice.

This time none of Don's fishing buddies wanted to join us, so we went solo. This was when there was no GPS or EPIRG equipment to show the location of the boat. Our only contact with the world was through the marine operator, but when we got to the fishing grounds we were out of range, so there was no one we could contact at all. Soon after we put the gear in, we found the fish, a lot of fish. Huge kings were hitting the lines one after the other. We were busy for hours cleaning and freezing the fish. It was kind of eerie because we were in this huge "bite" all by ourselves. This is what a fisherman dreams about. It was late in the season, mid-September, so the days were already a lot shorter.

Pretty soon we started to see the ocean swells increase, gently at first. The barometer quickly dropped, so we knew a good sized storm was on its way. We pulled up all the gear and headed for Lituya Bay, about a five-hour run. The other crewman, Lynn, and I latched everything down and headed inside the cabin. Right then the storm hit full on. The wind was screaming through the mast and the wires. The bow of the *Charbus* bravely dove right into these huge waves. This is when you find out just how seaworthy the boat is. I didn't have time to even think about getting seasick.

Suddenly the engine stopped, definitely not a good situation to be in. Don was swearing a streak of profanities as he ran down into the engine room. The bilge pump stopped, and the boat quickly filled up with water. Lynn and I took turns strapped to the hand pump on the back deck, pumping as fast as we could. We rode those huge waves rudderless as we had no engine to steer with. The boat turned so it was parallel to the waves no longer facing straight into them. Now the water crashed directly down onto the boat.

We stopped pumping because we couldn't keep up, and we were afraid we would get washed overboard.

At this point, I realized the odds of surviving this were not good. I went down to see if I could help Don in the engine room, but he was the only one who could figure out how to get the engine running again. So, I sat down at the galley table and started praying. Lynn sat across from me, and I began saying our last rites. I knew getting into a survival suit was the next step, but we were a long ways from shore and had no means of contacting anyone about our location. Finding us would be like finding a needle in a haystack. There was an amazing presence of clarity and calmness between us as we sat there with the storm raging outside. Suddenly we heard the engine sputter. We both jumped about a foot and rushed down to find out what was going on. Miraculously, Don got the engine running. It was so surreal to sit there, honestly believing it was the end. We bucked the storm all the way to Lituya Bay and just made it through the breakers before it was impassable to get into the bay with the tide going out. It was so wonderful to actually anchor up to something solid. We hadn't eaten or slept for over twenty-four hours. I had no idea how long we were out there in the storm. It was a weird sense of timelessness and felt like a different world.

I made a lot of money my first season fishing with Don. I left Alaska in late September of 1980 and headed back to the lower 48. I was not surprised to find out most of my friends left too, to warmer climates, usually south of the equator. I traveled a bit and went to see my family in Nebraska. I knew before I left Alaska I would be coming back to fish the next season, ready for more adventures.

The following spring, I took the Alaska Marine Highway ferry from Seattle to Sitka. This time I could afford to stay in a berth cabin. I knew some of my friends were "running" a boat out of Seattle up to Sitka for the seine season. I was hanging out on the stern watching the pristine landscape go by as we were about to go through the Narrows south of Petersburg, Alaska. Just before we got to town, I saw the boat. It was so hilarious because they saw me wave and every single one of them promptly turned around, dropped their pants, and mooned me. At this point, the ship began to list to one side after the captain announced what was going on. Several of the passengers rushed over to catch a glimpse of it. Welcome to Alaska!

When I got to Sitka, I started looking for a fishing job. This is when I met Ken, a fisherman who had invented an automatic baiting system which simplified the longline process for catching black cod. He was a successful fisherman as well and already had his crew for the season. It seemed there were no commercial fishing jobs available in Sitka.

My friend Nance had not found any work either. We came up with a plan to go north to Bristol Bay, Alaska, to look for a job on a gillnet boat. We got to Anchorage, Alaska and spent a couple days there. The city is surrounded by stunning snowcapped mountains. Lots of hiking and biking trails meander through town. We found the most economical way to fly to Naknek in Bristol Bay. Just as we were about to buy our plane tickets, the fishermen went on strike. It was impossible to predict when the strike would end, so we returned to Sitka.

Nance headed back to Petersburg, and I soon followed to look for work there. I got a job with the Alaska Forest Service surveying logging roads on Wrangell Island where the camp was based on Fools Inlet. One of the things required for the job was to know how to defend yourself if you encountered a bear. This meant I had to learn how to shoot a large rifle. Clearly, I was not in Kansas anymore, not even close.

Three weeks into the job, the survey site had moved farther up the mountain. This required a helicopter from Petersburg to transport us there. On some of those days, the visibility was not good, so we had to hike up to the location. One particular day, it was my turn to lead with the rifle. Halfway up the mountain, as I turned a corner on the trail, a very large brown bear stood with her two cubs, twenty feet away. I completely froze. Thank goodness, the rest of the crew appeared a split second later. All three bears turned around and left. That was the last time they asked me to carry the rifle. Near the camp a short boat ride away was Anan Creek, where a large run of salmon came up to spawn. This was one of the places where you could see a lot of black and brown bears. Of course I went with a group from camp to check it out. Watching them from a safe distance was absolutely incredible. I saw several black bears expertly picking up a salmon from the stream. Then all of a sudden they split. A very large brown bear appeared in the same spot and grabbed a salmon out of the river. We knew it was time to leave and go back to camp.

When the job ended a month later, I went to Nebraska to see my family and spend time with my sister Diane. I decided to go back to Sitka that spring. This was when Ken and I started spending more time together and fell in love. He had the *Elizabeth B*, a seventy-two-foot steel shrimper from the Gulf of Mexico to fish black cod and halibut during the seasons. There was a three-day halibut opening he and his crew had just outfitted for, and he asked me to join them. We headed up north past Baranof Island where we set out the halibut gear. They used an automated baiting system onboard the boat. The crew did not have to bait or snap on the gear by hand. Each set started and ended with a marker and a weight attached to place the gear at the depth the skipper wanted. The placement of the gear would hopefully attract the halibut so they would bite. By the time they finished all of the sets, the first one had soaked long enough. It was time to pull up the gear. I quickly learned halibut are strong fighters when they break the water or come on deck. They can range in size from fifty to several hundred pounds each. It took at least two strong crewmen to pull the halibut out of the water. Then watch out, they go crazy once they hit the deck.

On the second day of the opening, the ocean started to get choppy, and I got seasick. A part of me wanted to call the Coast Guard and tell them I wanted off that boat now. This was not an option. We were not in any danger, so I had to tough it out. No one could cook in the galley because nothing stayed on the countertop. It's risky just to open the refrigerator, so it was locked up. The only food we prepared were sandwiches in the sink. This went on for two days. I spent a lot of time on the back deck, looking out at the horizon. This was when the porpoises appeared, hundreds of them. They were on both sides of the boat and followed us to the next set. As I watched them swim in perfect unison, I was mesmerized. My seasickness stopped, and I was fine the rest of the trip.

After we got back to town, Ken's financial problems had gotten worse, and he lost his patent rights for the automatic longline system. The bank was threatening to take his boat and all the gear on it. A couple of days later, Ken decided to sneak out of the harbor in the middle of the night to avoid the confrontation. The harbor was packed since the halibut opening had just ended. The boat was tied up next to three other boats. It was the middle of June. There was still some light at midnight when we left the dock. It was just the two of us on the boat. In order to leave the dock, we had to wake up a couple of crewmen on the other boats to help us slip out of the harbor. We ran the boat to the other side of Baranof Island to rendezvous with another boat. His friends helped us take all the gear off and put it on their boat. The bank foreclosed on the *Elizabeth B* soon after we got back to town without the gear.

At the same time, my sister Diane was diagnosed with a rare form of cancer. I went back to Nebraska to be with her and my family as she courageously went through several rounds of chemo. It was a very difficult time for all of us. She passed away in November of 1981.

The night before she passed away, I had a vivid dream. In it, I walked alongside a stream with tall majestic trees that pointed up to a brilliant blue sky. Diane walked on the other side across from me. I looked over at her; she told me everything was going to be okay. When the dream ended, I woke up and bolted out of bed. It was early in the morning, maybe 4 A.M. or 5 A.M. I got dressed and went straight to the hospital to see her. Just as I walked into her room, she stopped breathing. I saw that dream as her way of signaling to me she was no longer here but in a beautiful, peaceful place somewhere out there in the universe, and not to worry.

When you lose a loved one, no matter what the circumstances, it is devastating. What got me through it was my family, friends, and my faith. I felt God's deep love embraced and comforted me as I mourned the loss of my sister. I had watched Diane's faith flourish significantly during her illness, too. This gave me the strength to get through this difficult time. I knew I was not alone; she was with me. My sister was no longer suffering.

Soon after the funeral in Nebraska, I returned to Sitka. It was full on winter; the mountains were blanketed with radiant white snow. Many of the fishermen had taken their boats south to Seattle or Bellingham, Washington. The town was quiet with not much activity going on. Ken had leased a small boat called the *Cape Strait* from a friend of his. He had designed a pot for shrimping so we built over a dozen of them in his friend's work shed. A couple weeks later we went out shrimping in the bays around Baranof Island.

For whatever reason, I did not cry much at my sister's funeral. But after a day of shrimping when we anchored up for the night, I cried a lot. I sat on the back deck of the boat cradled by the pristine landscape with the quiet sounds of the water. This is when I finally allowed myself to grieve. One of the nights I sat out there, the water around the boat glowed a bright phosphorescent pale green. I had never seen anything like it before. I just sat there mesmerized, in awe of this natural beauty that gently surrounded me.

Ken was very patient with me and did most of the work on those trips, including the cooking. On one of them we saw an eagle fly by the boat just above the water. There was a huge splash as the eagle latched onto a good sized coho salmon. The eagle's wings flapped wildly until it landed on a rock and released it. At this point, Ken skillfully maneuvered toward the rock, scared the eagle away, and picked up the fish. That night we had delicious coho salmon for dinner.

On another fishing trip, we had been running for about an hour going north through a small narrows located at the top of Baranof Island. There is a nice bay on the other side where Ken wanted to go ashore and hunt for deer. It was slack tide, so it was easy to let the boat idle instead of anchoring it. I stayed onboard while Ken got in the small skiff and rowed to shore to hunt. After a couple of hours had gone by, the tide was quickly coming in. He had tied the skiff to a rock on the shore, but it had come loose and was floating out into the bay. I knew Ken did not know how to swim and the water was frigid cold. Now I was in high gear, formulating a solution to get Ken back to the boat. When he got back to the beach, he was dragging a nice sized buck that he had shot.

At this point, I began to maneuver the boat over to the skiff and was able to grab it, pulling it alongside the boat. I guided it a little closer to the shore and put it in idle. Then I got in the skiff and rowed to shore to pick up Ken and the deer. Once they were in the skiff, I rowed back to the boat that was still in the same spot. As a little added drama to all of this, some blood from the deer dripped over the sides of the skiff into the water. Like a scene out of a film, two white fins quietly appeared right next to the skiff. The two orcas' fins rose out of the water, completely in sync with us. Miraculously we made it back to the boat safely. We headed to the fishing grounds to shrimp on the east side of the Baranof Island.

As the year went by, I was happy to be in love with Ken but quite naïve about exactly what I had gotten myself into. He had separated from his wife when we got together. I knew he loved me very much, but early on I started to notice signs our relationship was not a solid, healthy one. He had been a successful fisherman and inventor, but financial problems had been going on before we met. More and more, Ken would frequently drink a lot when we were in town, but there was never any alcohol on the boat, nor did he drink when we were out fishing. I did not understand in the beginning it would become a serious problem. I was in love with him and thought it was something I could fix.

In the summer of 1982, we decided to fish the three-day halibut opening. The crew was my friend Nance and me. The rest of the fishing fleet thought we would not catch much, given that the crew was two women, and Ken had an injured foot, but they were wrong. Since it was a short opening, everyone, including us, fished nonstop for the three days. Ken found the fish early the first day, and it never slowed down. The halibut we caught averaged around 200 to 400 pounds each. It took all three of us just to get one halibut in. Once it hit the deck, they went wild and flopped all over the place. In about forty-eight hours we had filled up the hold with halibut.

Ken sped up the engine and headed back to Sitka to sell the fish. Rock and roll music boomed over the speakers while Nance and I finished cleaning and icing the rest of the halibut. All of us were exhausted but so happy we had just filled the boat with fish, a successful trip so far. Soon, after we left the fishing grounds, Ken slowed the boat down. Just as it leveled out, we heard a loud sloshing sound. We opened up the floorboards in the galley and saw water rushing in. The bilge pump was not keeping up. We were sinking.

Of all the situations to be in, especially with Nance— wow. Amazingly, it was a warm midsummer's day. The ocean was flat calm, and the shore was clearly visible about half a mile away. We had three survival suits on board. Both Nance and I knew how to swim, but Ken did not. We started to toss some of the fish from the hold into the ocean to lighten the weight of the boat.

Immediately, Ken sent out a "Mayday" call on the radio to the Coast Guard. They quickly responded and dispatched a helicopter to our location. We were a couple hours running time from Sitka where they were based. When it arrived, they circled around the boat and dropped a metal can into the ocean close to us to retrieve. It was a challenge to get it onboard. Inside of the can was a pump. The whole thing played out like a scene in a movie. The three of us stood there looking down at this dusty pump that had obviously not been used for a while. We pulled it out and set it up to begin pumping out the water, but it did not start. We sat there at the galley table going through the directions trying to figure out why. After several minutes, Nance calmly read through the directions, step by step. Toward the bottom of the list, they said you have to prime the pump before it can start. After Ken did this, the pump started right up, pushing water out of the boat. This is what kept the boat afloat until we got to Sitka.

It was a slow ride back, but we made it. After all the fish were unloaded at the cold storage, the wood boat was hauled out of the water to take a closer look and figure out what the problem was. The next day, Ken found a small hole in the stern. The boat was repaired a day later, so we were able to go back out for a couple of days to finish up the rest of the halibut opening.

On the first leg of the trip, I got a little seasick, which was unusual since we had not been in any storms at sea. When we finished up the halibut season, I knew something was going on with me. After I went to the doctor to get everything checked out, the tests came back. The reason I had gotten sick was because I was pregnant. I was so happy and excited about this news. Ken was happy too, but it seemed like his drinking was getting worse. This is when our relationship began to have problems. I went back to Nebraska a couple of times to visit family and seriously thought about leaving Ken, but I still wanted to give him, the father of our child, another chance. I returned to Sitka around Christmastime, in December of 1982.

I took Lamaze classes by myself because Ken was usually out fishing and had no interest in going with me. One of the classes focused on C-sections. I was in pretty good health and decided to skip it, assuming everything would go smoothly, but a C-section is exactly what happened.

During this time, we were in the Pioneer Bar with the rest of his crew. Ken was playing pool with his buddy Mike and suddenly Ken threw a punch at Mike. I don't know what the hell I was thinking, but I stood in between them to break it up and I was a good seven months pregnant. A giant beam of light went off in my head. I knew that I did not and could not handle what was going on with Ken. He had a serious drinking problem, and I finally realized I could not fix it.

Around the baby's due date, my Mom came up to Sitka to be with me. I went into the hospital on Saturday, March 19 to have the baby. There were only two of us in the entire the hospital. I started out in the birthing room, but some complications arose, and I was quickly prepped for a C-section. It was the weekend, so a lot of people were out sport fishing, including the anesthesiologist. He quickly got back to town while the doctor and nurses got me ready.

When you have a C-section, they do not put you completely under; it's called twilight, so you are still a little bit aware of what is going on. I had a vision of looking down at myself as my son was being born. Standing right next to me was my sister, Diane. This was my second experience in the spirit world with her.

My beautiful son Nolan had arrived. When we were released from the hospital, we went back to the live-aboard boat where Ken and I stayed when we were in town. Now it was very clear to me: I could not deal with Ken's drinking and raise a child at the same time. He was an alcoholic. I gave Ken an ultimatum—either he stopped drinking and went into treatment, or we were going to leave. He told me he was not going to stop. A couple of weeks later, Nolan and I got on a plane and left Sitka, Alaska for good. We moved to Nebraska to be near my family and start our new life.

4

Following My Dream

As more memories rose to the surface, I discovered parts of my life were intrinsically connected, revealing important key events that led me to a remarkable career. This chapter is a glimpse into that journey I have been on for most of my adult life—one I will always cherish and hold dear.

Nolan and I left Alaska in April 1983 to begin our new life in Lincoln, Nebraska. I knew coming back home was the right decision; being surrounded by supportive family and friends was an essential step for both of us. Once we got settled in, I got a part time office job at Theisen Brothers.. They had a small office in Lincoln, so I was able to bring Nolan with me to work, and he could spend some time with his grandfather. I was grateful to have this job in this familiar setting while I figured out what the next step was for us.

Deep down, I knew my passion for films was still very much alive. The same PBS station, NET, where I had applied for a job five years earlier after I graduated from college, was still there. Not getting the job then, propelled me down a completely different path, spurring me to explore new adventures. This led me to southeast Alaska and commercial fishing. My friend Jenny was the one who told me about it and had friends to help us find work once we arrived in Sitka. When I got to her place in Idaho, she had changed her mind. My sister Diane found out and asked her friend, Steve to meet me in Seattle. We both got on the Alaska Marine Highway ferry that took us up through the Inside Passage to our destination. A lot had transpired since that first interview at NET, but I felt it was a good place to start.

Soon after Nolan turned two, I applied for a position on their camera crew and got the job. I was really excited to get my foot in the door. NET was one of the PBS stations that produced a variety of shows, including sports, opera, classical music, documentaries, and historical dramas. The level of production they were doing was pretty impressive, and I was very happy to be a part of it. With a full-time job, Nolan was in daycare during the week either with my mom or friends from church. Most of the time, he was with our dear friends, Lynn and Jim and their family.

The first year on the camera crew flew by quickly. I really enjoyed being part of a large crew doing the setup work and operating a camera during a shoot. I soon realized my interest was on the producing side. There was an associate producer position in the cultural affairs unit. I applied for and got that job. My responsibilities were assisting the producer on shows done in our unit. This varied from organizing a shoot with the camera crew, to sitting in the control truck next to the director calling out camera shots during live performances, to helping the editor.

At the end of the first year, I had the opportunity to direct a short documentary about the University of Nebraska's remarkable Barkley Center, which focuses on special education and communication disorders. It was an incredible moving experience to meet and interview some of the teachers, parents, and children involved in their program. Outside of work at the station, I really enjoyed working with my friend Roselle on developing a story about commercial fishing in southeast Alaska. The main character, Kate, a successful artist living in Chicago, returns home after she finds out her dad had tragically and mysteriously died while he was out commercial fishing.

One of the most challenging projects our unit produced was the docudrama about the great Ponca Chief Standing Bear, called *The Trial of Standing Bear*. It traces the journey he and his family made from Oklahoma to their homeland in Nebraska during the frigid winter of 1879. The story centers on an historic federal court case that became one of the most pivotal moments in the history of our country for Native Americans. Chief Standing Bear won, giving him, the Ponca people, and all Native American tribes full rights as citizens of the United States. They were no longer wards of the federal government.

This was my first full-fledged film production, bringing cast and crew from other parts of the country and Los Angeles to Lincoln, Nebraska, to work on it with us. We had a couple months of prep to build sets, hold tryouts for actors and extras, and location scouting before we started shooting. I worked alongside the first assistant director, Bob, as the second assistant director, working closely with the director, producer, line producer, director of photography, actors, and crew. Most of them had worked on large film productions before, making it an invaluable experience for me. Things started to click. Being a part of that creative process was exactly what I wanted to do.

In January of 1988, I took a week off to attend my first Sundance Film Festival. It was still a relatively small festival, showing mostly foreign and independent films. I was thrilled to be in this environment, watching two or three films a day that usually had an unconventional approach rather than a linear storyline. This was the style of filmmaking I preferred. Besides watching films, there were other events going on throughout the festival. I attended several roundtable discussions with the actors and the director that were inspiring. I went the following year, too. This experience, along with working on the docudrama, propelled me closer to the next step in my career.

I kept in touch with friends from film school who were now living in San Francisco, California, and working in production throughout the Bay Area. I was able to take another week off to visit them and discuss what their experiences in the film industry had been so far. I simply asked them if I moved to the Bay Area with my son, would they help me get production work? They all said yes and encouraged me to go for it!

The torch had been lit. It was time to embark on the next part of my journey, to pursue a career in feature films. As soon as I got back home, I discussed moving to the Bay Area with my parents. They were skeptical about this idea, especially since I did not have a job lined up yet. They reminded me that even though I had done things like this in the past, the circumstances now were quite different. An essential, integral part of this plan was what was best for Nolan.

Part of my decision to do this was based on the frequent trips we had made the last five years to visit Grandad and Minnie, in Sebastopol, California, an hour north of San Francisco. We were already familiar with the North Bay and had always enjoyed spending time there. I discussed my plan with them to see what they thought about it. They were excited and graciously offered to let us live with them until we got situated.

A couple of months later, during the summer of 1989, Nolan and I packed the car and drove west to California. With my grandparents' help and support, along with that of my friends in the city, things began to click. I got freelance production jobs at a variety of companies in San Francisco. Each one gave me a unique production experience and helped build a network of contacts in the film industry.

Our home base at Grandad and Minnie's was a godsend. There were so many new things for us to adjust to but such a great comfort to have their help and advice to navigate us through them. Living with them also meant Nolan had more time with his great grandfather, who was a retired teacher. He often volunteered in Nolan's classroom. When there were sports events or practices after school, Grandad took care of the transportation when I had to work.

Minnie had moved from a small village on Lake Lugano in Northern Italy with her family when she was a little girl. She was an excellent cook. We were welcomed into her large extended family and celebrated many holidays with them. Traditional American food was served, but the highlight was her homemade ravioli with several other Northern Italian dishes. And there were the desserts she made from scratch. For the chocolate chip cookies, she used walnuts from her friend's tree down the road. This involved Grandad and Nolan, too. They sat out in the back patio and cracked the walnuts. The cookie jar was always full of a fresh batch when you walked through their kitchen.

The routine we had at their house was wonderful. It was important to have a daily schedule of activities. Before we moved there, Grandad had bought several lovely children's books for Nolan to read to him. He continued this when we lived with them. After dinner, we often played a card or board game. Usually friends or family would stop by and join us. It was always a lot of fun. One of our favorite games we played a lot was Rummikub. After Nolan and I moved into our own place in town, we frequently stopped by to play. It was a nice way to unwind from a long day at work.

They lived in the country on a beautiful acreage just outside of town. Grandad called it "Shangri-La." There was a large apple orchard and a bay leaf tree where Minnie got the bay leaves for her pasta sauces. Next to the house was a lemon tree she used to make her delicious lemon meringue pie. In the fall we picked persimmons from the trees in front of the house and let them ripen. When they were ready, they tasted very sweet, like dessert.

Every year they planted a large garden with lots of fresh vegetables, which included artichokes. This was my introduction to steamed artichokes dipped in butter. Of course there was sweet corn too. Grandad planted the seeds in stages so we had fresh corn on the cob all summer long. Deep purple grapes hung off the rooftop of the barn with plenty of strawberries, blackberries, and raspberries underneath. Next to the barn were the snap peas that cascaded down the metal fence. There was an automatic alarm clock when the rooster crowed in the mornings. We always had fresh eggs from the hens. Life in the country with them that first year was a special time for us. I certainly did not miss the frigid cold winters and hot summers of Nebraska.

One of the many things we were introduced to in California was the beach and professional sports teams, specifically baseball. Grandad was an avid sports fan. He organized trips to the Oakland A's games with a group from the Senior Center in Santa Rosa. We often went with them on the bus to the games. Grandad taught Nolan how the game was played. He already had a keen interest in the sport early on because he had been named after Nolan Ryan, the pitcher for the Texas Rangers. Spending time at those games deepened his appreciation and love for the sport. Football was the other sport we paid attention to. Honestly, if you grew up in Nebraska like we did, odds are you are a big Cornhusker fan. Often Saturday afternoons during football season were spent outside underneath the towering redwood tree. We cheered on the Nebraska Cornhuskers with Grandad as we listened on his old radio.

A couple of months after we moved to Sebastopol, the Oakland A's played the San Francisco Giants in the 1989 World Series. Locals called it the Bay Series. The A's were two games ahead in the series. The day they played game three, I was home watching it with Nolan. We had just sat down for dinner to watch the pregame show when suddenly everything began to shake. I jumped up to look out the large plate glass windows in the dining room and froze as I saw the trees go parallel to the ground with a loud whooshing sound. I glanced up at the sky. It was clear blue with brilliant sunshine. There was no tornado in sight. As I stood there perplexed, the back door slammed shut. My son had run outside, and I quickly followed him. There was a humming-bird feeder on the steps swaying wildly back and forth. This was when it became crystal clear what had just happened. Somehow my son had done exactly what you were supposed to do in this situation.

This happened on October 17, 1989, when a magnitude 6.9 earthquake, called the Loma Prieta, rocked the entire Bay Area. This was one of the rare times Grandad and Minnie were out of town, so we were home by ourselves. Thank goodness I did not have a job in the city that day. The epicenter was located in the Santa Cruz Mountains south of San Francisco. Parts of the city were damaged, especially in the Marina district and several of the bridges. We were sixty miles north of the Bay area in Sonoma County, far enough away to have minimal damage. Over the twenty-two years I lived in California, I experienced several small earthquakes; none of them were even close to the strength and magnitude of this one. What an introduction to the Golden State, our new home.

The following year, we attended several baseball games with Grandad and Minnie and the group from the senior center. It was nice to ride with them on the bus and arrive early enough to watch the players warm up. An hour before the game started, fans were allowed to stand near the team's dugout where some of the players signed baseball cards. My enthusiastic seven-year-old son patiently waited to get one of his cards signed. A couple of times he was engulfed by a throng of older, taller fans as they reached over him to get their cards signed. Talk about an anxious parent. Often players saw my son underneath all that craziness and tried to sign his card first.

My friend John found out Nolan Ryan was scheduled to pitch for the Rangers at the Oakland A's game on June 11, 1990. I made sure we could go, and John got the tickets. We were told by a couple of people that he did not sign baseball cards at the game. Nolan neatly wrote a letter that explained he was named after him and would be at the game with his mom to watch him pitch. He enclosed his favorite baseball card with the letter. I overnighted it to the Texas Ranger's office in Arlington two days before the game. The next day they overnighted a response from Nolan Ryan with the baseball card signed the day before the game. This was the beginning of an incredible experience for my son.

Early in the game, the Ranger's took the lead. Around the fifth inning, the A's had not scored. John told my son it was time to rally the teams. He slid his Oakland A's cap around and Nolan did the same with his Texas Rangers' cap. When the seventh inning began, fans started to chant

"Nolan." My son's eyes widened as the entire stadium became electrified cheering Nolan Ryan on. They sensed what was about to happen. We witnessed a slice of baseball history on that day when Nolan Ryan pitched his sixth no-hitter. My son was jubilant to have watched his namesake pitch such a memorable game. This insured his loyalty as a fan to the Texas Rangers.

Later that summer, I checked in with my friend Jim about possible jobs at George Lucas's company, Industrial Light and Magic, where he worked. I had applied for a couple of jobs earlier but did not get one. Now there was a two-week job in September to set up interviews for visual effects technical directors to work on the film *Terminator 2*. This time I got the job.

The knowledge I had about ILM at this point was that it had started in 1975 as part of George Lucas's production company, Lucasfilm, for the sole purpose of creating special effects for the first three *Star Wars* films. ILM was in San Rafael, a half hour from his ranch on Lucas Valley Road. When I went there for an interview the first time, it was a challenge just to find the place. I knew it was the correct address, but written on the front door was Kerner Optical Lab, not ILM. I found out later this nondescript name kept the location under the radar.

After I walked through the front door of D Building, I saw the iconic magician logo with ILM written underneath prominently placed on the wall by the front desk. Down the first hallway were several movie posters of films they had worked on and two impressive miniature models framed in glass. What ILM was all about began to sink in. As I got further down the hallway, there was a crew busy filming, on one of the stages, a miniature model of the submarine for the film *The Hunt for Red October*. It felt like I had entered the inner sanctum where the magic happened.

The interviews I scheduled were done through a land-line telephone because cell phones were not as available as they are today. The candidates were scattered in places around the world from Australia to Canada, France, and Germany, which meant the time difference had to be factored in. All the positons were quickly filled a couple of weeks later. When we finished, I thought my job was done at ILM, but they offered me a production assistant position in the VFX department. I was so excited to have work for another year. This was thanks to one of my schoolmates from college, Jim, who was a key part in my getting the job.

At The Ground Level

In September of 1990, my career in feature films began at ILM. I was excited, ready to dive into my production assistant position in the newly formed visual effects department. Step by step, my previous production experiences in freelancing and NET, the PBS station in Nebraska, had given me a solid basis to work from, but this job was a completely different part of the filmmaking process. No doubt about it, I had a steep learning curve ahead of me. The tech staff set me up with my first computer, an Apple Macintosh, and gave me a crash course on how to use it. My typing skills were minimal, so I took the Mavis Beacon online course on the weekends to improve. Part of my job was typing up notes and sending them out to the crew regarding the shots in progress that had been reviewed in the morning "dailies" by the VFX supervisor. The terminology used sounded like a foreign language, very esoteric and specific. It took me a while to absorb this and understand the intricacies in the realm of visual effects work. A strong sense of camaraderie developed as we ventured out into the emerging world of VFX.

The overall process used in visual effects was to shoot a live action plate shot on location with a 35-mm camera. This was then processed and scanned into a digital format for the editor to cut in to a scene in the film. When the director approved the shot, it was then turned over to the vendor, ILM. The digital plate was put online where the visual effects elements were created to put into the plate, which became the final shot. This process generated complex imagery from environments to creatures, or it could have been a straightforward composite putting two plates together. The results that ended up on the big screen were always stunningly realistic.

The work ILM did on *Terminator 2*, was a small amount, but it was groundbreaking at that time. Soon after it was released in 1991, directors began to incorporate more VFX into their films. Step by step, ILM kept pace with these new opportunities in the film industry. The company quickly expanded and brought in more top-notch talent from different parts of the world.

Those early days of VFX were an amazing time. It was thrilling to be a part of the sheer magnitude and speed at which the technology developed and accelerated. I had a front row seat. After T2 wrapped in May 1991, they put me on another film, the first *Jurassic Park*. At this point, I thought we should move to San Rafael, closer to ILM. My commute in the morning was already an hour and a half on a good day, making my job a twelve- to thirteen-hour day. I asked my son what he thought about this idea. Right away, he told me he did not want to move. His quick response made me understand more clearly how hard it had been for him to leave friends and family in Lincoln. We had only been in Sebastopol for a year, which is a short period of time to make big adjustments to a new home, new school, and new friends. To ask my seven-year-old son to make all those changes again was too much.

Honestly, deep down I knew it would be difficult to move again. My sweet, wise son helped me make the decision to stay. Granddad and Minnie continued to be an integral part of our lives. Our new friends we had met the first year became part of our extended family too. All those relationships enriched our lives in ways beyond anything I could have envisioned. Nolan and I have been greatly blessed with these dear friendships over all these many years. We spent the next fifteen years in beautiful Sebastopol, California.

His response was a wake-up call for me because I had been so focused on getting my career going that I had not slowed down to think through how much it had affected my son. These were very formative years for him. It was important for me to find the balance between work and what was best for my son. On weekends and holidays, we did things together, whether they were sports events, trips to visit family, or travel abroad. I greatly cherished those years as I watched my son flourish into a wonderful young man. He always keeps me grounded and is one of my greatest joys.

My job was never a typical 9-to-5 day; it always involved long hours. Add to this, being a single mom did not make it any easier. There were not many people in my situation at ILM. In fact I was the only one. When I got my next job on *Jurassic Park*, the head of production asked me if they could count on me to work the long hours and weekends required until the show wrapped. Of course, I told them yes, they could count on me. The journey to pursue my dream to work on feature films had begun.

With the possibility of more consistent work at ILM, I felt it was really important to go back to visit family in Nebraska a least a couple times a year. When Nolan was in grade school and off for the summers, either Grandad or I traveled back to Lincoln so he could spend a month with his grandmother, keeping him involved and connected with family and friends. Even though he was a huge Rangers fan already, his passion for the Nebraska Cornhuskers also shaped him early on in his life.

In the film *Jurassic Park*, more groundbreaking VFX work was done. The director, Steven Spielberg, wanted to use close-up shots of the T-Rex chasing the jeep down a road in one of the scenes. The life-size practical animatronic puppet model had limitations and could not achieve the kind of action shots Steven wanted. ILM got to work and developed the first computer-generated model or CGI of the T-Rex along with several other dinosaurs. On the screen, those shots looked and felt like a full-sized living, breathing T-Rex. Both worked seamlessly together to create a terrifying series of shots in that scene. What was developed in CGI for this film further broadened the use of VFX and the floodgates opened.

After *Jurassic Park*, released in June of 1993, I got on another show, *Baby's Day Out*, as one of the production coordinators. I had a little bit more flexibility, so when it was not too busy, which was rare, the producer let me leave work early. It was such a treat because I was able to go to some of Nolan's baseball games. When he got a little bit older, I often brought him to work with me on Saturdays. There were plenty of places for him to explore. He went to dailies with me and got to know a lot of the artists working on the show, which included the model shop where they built miniatures. Sometimes he hung out with the stage crew and watched them set up and shoot miniatures on one of the stages. My son was never bored; he thoroughly enjoyed spending time with me at work.

When ILM started as a company, people were hired, project to project. Those in upper management had salaried positions. Usually, this meant a month or two off in between films. With the growth of visual effects, there was work year round. Many of us who had started on T2 stayed at ILM and moved up the production ladder. The company provided health care and 401K retirement funds which they contributed to. After each show, a t-shirt and a movie poster for the film was given to each person who worked at the company. I was really impressed and happy to work for a company like ILM, which took really good care of their employees along with all of the other companies George Lucas had. We were all part of a large extended family.

Each year, Lucasfilm and ILM put on several events, from holiday parties to wrap parties to film screenings. Several well-known bands performed at these events and were never announced beforehand. The most memorable Christmas party for me was held in San Francisco at the Bill Graham Civic Auditorium. When the stage lit up, Los Lobos went right in to one of their classic songs. Everyone cut loose on the dance floor!

At the Halloween party, the costumes were incredibly inventive, especially the ones worn by people who worked in the art department and the model shop. Awards were given out for the best costume. One year Jonathan from the art department made a larger-than-life-size monster head that seemed to float above his shoulder. He won the prize that year. Another big event was the Fourth of July picnic at the Ranch. This was the one time my family came out from Nebraska to go with us. The day was filled with a variety of activities and wonderful food, which included an ice cream truck. We always participated in the egg toss and the one-legged race. To add to the festivities, a lot of George's family and friends in the film business attended.

The first time I went on location was as the VFX production coordinator for the film *Daylight* in January of 1995. Most of it was shot at Cinecitta Studios, outside of Rome,

Italy. The studio, was legendary for many reasons. It was built during Benito Mussolini's reign in 1937 to make propaganda films during WW II and was bombed by Western Allies. Eventually, it was rebuilt in the early 1950s. This was the period of time when the Italian film industry flourished. Several of my favorite directors, from Federico Fellini to Bernardo Bertolucci, made films there.

As I mentioned before, I had been in Rome once during a tour of Europe in the summer of 1972 with students from my high school. Of all the places we visited, Rome was one of my favorite cities. I still vividly remember going to the Trevi Fountain on the last day we were there. The tradition was to throw a coin into the fountain with your right hand as you tossed it over your left shoulder. If you did this, it guaranteed you would return to Rome. I was one of the many tourists who did that. Little did I know then, I would be back to work on a feature film twenty-three years later.

It was great to be back in Rome, but this time it meant being away from Nolan for at least two months. I missed him so much. It was really hard for me. I knew he was fine living with the Gurule family while I was away. This was the family he stayed with after school since I started at ILM six years earlier. Neither one of us had cell phones, so it was not possible to text or Skype with Nolan, plus it was a nine-hour time difference. I called him in the morning on the landline at the hotel on my day off. It was always wonderful to hear his voice and get an update on what was going on with him.

Scott, the VFX supervisor, strongly recommended we stay at a hotel in the old part of Rome instead of outside the city near the studio. It was a brilliant idea. We found a place near the subway line that went out to the studio. When you go on location, the production coordinator's responsibilities are a bit different than post-production. On the first day, as usual, I walked ahead of the crew, thinking I should keep up the pace, so we got to the subway in time to catch the early train. I was about to turn the corner and go down the steps to the subway when I looked behind me to make sure everyone was there. No, they were not. Scott was missing. I could hear his voice in the distance speaking in broken Italian. He had walked into the kitchen of a restaurant we had just passed to discuss what they were serving for dinner that night. The rest of the crew already knew what he was doing; they had all worked on location with him before. They totally cracked up when they saw the bewildered look on my face. I learned early on, you go with the flow.

Each morning on our way to the subway, we took different routes so Scott could check out restaurants along the way to decide where we were going to dinner that night. This is how I discovered lots of wonderful Italian dishes during the two months I was there. One of the dishes I often had with the main course was spinaci, fresh spinach sautéed in garlic and virgin olive oil. Yum. At the end of the meal, I always had a dessert. My favorite was tiramisu. Each place we went to had its own delicious version of it. One thing about eating out in Rome I really enjoyed was the atmosphere in the restaurants. We were never rushed, always felt relaxed. It was a nice way to end a long day of filming. This was where I was introduced to caffe macchiato, the real one, which is still my favorite cup of coffee. The food served at the studio commissary was good too. One of my favorite dishes was gnocchi on Fridays.

I learned a lot on this show regarding the physical production side of filmmaking, which was different from pre-production and post-production. The majority of the VFX work was budgeted based on the script. Once the work was awarded, the VFX plates were shot on location. During the shoot, the goal was to stick to the shooting schedule, but there were always changes and adjustments made on a daily basis. When it involved us, details pertinent to VFX changes had to be noted and written down for the VFX supervisor to discuss with the VFX producer, who was in San Rafael, California. It was important to always be aware of what was going on and keep everyone on our crew in the loop and informed. This was the one aspect of production that fascinated me. I felt like I was in my element.

After a couple of weeks, I had my routine down. On my one day off, after I visited with Nolan, I set out to explore the city. Rome was a very different city in January. Instead of throngs of tourists, there were mainly locals around. When I visited the well-known places in the city like the Sistine Chapel, it was completely empty, and I had the place to myself. Often I would go there to spend time in quiet prayer and contemplation as I admired Michelangelo's stunning masterpiece above me. I usually went to mass on Sunday at one of the churches in the old part of the city and always lit a candle for guardian angels to watch over and protect Nolan and my family.

Erika, my dear friend, was on location in Europe on another film for ILM at the same time. She came to visit me for a weekend, and we had a blast touring the old parts of the city. Rome has a Mediterranean climate similar to northern California, which was moderate with plenty of rain in the wintertime. We got soaked a couple of times, but we took in the lushness of the Villa Borghese's many beautiful gardens. Near the park is the top of the Spanish Steps. From there we had a stunning panoramic view of the city before we headed down the steps to the Piazza di Spagna. A couple streets off the piazza was a well-established local bar called Antica Enoteca, a perfect place for us to sit down and enjoy a glass of wine at the picturesque nineteenth-century wooden bar. They sold these exquisite glass-blown carafes, which I was tempted to buy.

The same day we visited the Pantheon, one of the architectural wonders in the city. The interior was completely open with a small dome in the center. Even though the rain was coming down in buckets outside, when we walked inside, there was not one drop of water on the floor. It was bone dry. One of the unique things about Rome was available drinking water. The fresh water was piped into these elegant fountains came from mountain rivers and flowed into the aqueducts around the city. The one next to my hotel was the Quattro Fontane fountains, one on each corner of this narrow street.

People were more sophisticated in how they dressed and in their mannerisms than what I was familiar with in northern California. And there were the cats. The books I saw about them treated them like the other residents of the city. Usually, I saw them around well-known places like the Colosseum and the Roman Forum, napping in the sun or nonchalantly sauntering past me. It was hilarious.

The period of time our crew spent on location was determined by the film producer. Those decisions were based on changes in the schedule or, for us, it was additional VFX work, which was why I ended up in Rome a couple weeks longer than planned. It was way too long for me to be gone from my son. When I got back home, I discussed this with him and chose not to go on location again unless it was a short period of time or when he was in college.

After I finished this show, I was given an opportunity to move up to a VFX associate producer position on the first *Men in Black*. There was a substantial amount of VFX work awarded to ILM, so two teams were assigned to the show. I was on the team with Ed, who was the VFX supervisor. The film had a lot of dry comical bits throughout, especially in the Headquarter Surveillance Egg Unit sequences our team worked on.

Most of the films we worked on at ILM were summer or Thanksgiving/Christmas releases. This worked well for me because I was able to take time off when Nolan was out of school. I certainly needed that break to relax and spend time with my son. When he was in high school, we took educational tours throughout Europe and Australia with some of his classmates and their parents. Those trips were so much fun and broadened my son's understanding and appreciation of other countries and cultures.

My next assignment at ILM was *Meet Joe Black* in the summer of 1998. A large portion of the film was shot in New York City. Michael, the VFX supervisor, and I were there on the first day of shooting on location at the intersection of 72nd Street and Lexington Avenue on the Upper Eastside of Manhattan. The shot involved Brad Pitt's character walking across four lanes of traffic and getting hit by a car. Just the logistics alone on any day of a shoot was a challenge but this was the first day, plus it was the most dramatic shot in the entire film, which happened to be one of our VFX shots. The area where we set-up our 35mm cameras was cordoned off from outside the perimeter of the intersection where paparazzi and onlookers were stationed to hopefully get a glimpse of the actors, specifically Brad.

Our little enclave was smack in the middle of that craziness. After we got the cameras ready to shoot the plate, it felt like a quiet oasis. As we waited for the rest of the crew to prep the cars and do the walk-through for the shot, this guy came over to me and introduced himself, "Hi, I'm Brad." As I shook Brad Pitt's hand, I just remember telling myself that I had no idea how incredibly handsome he was in person, plus he was down to earth and kind. He hung out with us along with his Irish bodyguards until we finished shooting the shot.

Moving up to the Big League

The next big project at ILM was *Star Wars: Episode 1—The Phantom Menace*, the first of the prequels, released in 1999. George Lucas wrote and directed this one. The film began with Luke Skywalker as a young boy and how his life unfolds through a complex series of relationships and machinations occurring in a galaxy far, far away. The pressure was certainly felt by everyone involved in this film, particularly at ILM. We were well aware of the remarkable fan base that had anxiously anticipated this film since *Star Wars: Episode VI—Return of the Jedi* came out in 1983.

The VFX work was divided into three units. I was put on the one with John and Judith, the VFX supervisor and producer as associate producer. Early on, Judith had to leave the show, so management moved me into the VFX producer position soon after I had started on the show. I told Dennis, one of the VFX supervisors, who had worked with George on the first three Star Wars, that I had only seen the third film, *Star Wars: Episode VI—Return of the Jedi*, not the first two. The wheels were turning. He looked at me, not in disbelief, but with the realization I was probably not the only one on the show who had not. Dennis called George to ask him if he could send prints of the three Star Wars films to ILM. He graciously agreed. The following week, we screened them in C theater, the largest one, with the THX sound system. It was great to watch the films in sequential order. This gave me a broader insight into the characters and a visual of the look that had been established. We were more than ready to get started on the next chapter of the Star Wars saga.

A couple of the sequences our unit worked on required additional people dotted throughout the frame in some of the shots. John discussed with George how he planned to do this. He wanted the extras to be people from our unit, dressed in the appropriate costumes to shoot the action for the shot in front of a blue screen on one of the stages at ILM. It turned out that several of us ended up in shots that are some of the sequences our unit worked on, particularly in the pod-race scene. There are some close-up shots of me sitting in the crowd.

At some level, ILM touched almost every shot in the film, whether it was a small adjustment to young Luke's eyes or to clean up or add something to the background in a shot. The experience of working on one of the Star Wars films was a dream come true for a lot of the people at ILM. This included the VFX supervisor, John. Maybe that was partly why our unit did the largest number of shots on the film. We were all happy to oblige to help make this a memorable experience for him and everyone on the show.

Dailies were part of every show I worked on at ILM, but this time it was different. When George and his producer, Rick, reviewed the shots for our unit, the comments were quick and thorough. And if he wanted changes to a shot, it was a given that the VFX producer—me—was ready to give him a general approximation of what it would cost. This was a little unnerving in the beginning, but it was so refreshing to have the director and producer right there making changes on the fly during dailies.

Of all the shows I had worked on so far, this was the biggest one. It involved a lot of long hours and weekends, but it was such an extraordinary experience to be a part of. I learned a great deal about what it means to be a VFX producer on this show. One of the important parts of this job was to stay on top of all the changes, every single one, and keep everyone informed and in sync between me, John, the crew, and my exceptional production team. The kind of situations and problem-solving I faced as a VFX producer, cannot be taught. It has to be learned through experience when you work on lots of films. I learned when to follow my intuition. This certainly prepped me for the next project, which was a much bigger challenge and a thrill to work on.

Star Wars: Episode 1—The Phantom Menace was released in the United States on May 23, 1999. It was the culmination of an extensive amount of VFX work everyone was proud of. So many people at ILM were involved in some capacity on this film. Nolan and I went to one of the family and friends screenings in San Francisco. Some of the press were there, and fans were lined up outside the theater when we walked in. After we saw the film, George gave a huge party for all of us to celebrate.

The following year, the film was nominated for best visual effects. This meant the VFX supervisors John, Dennis, Scott, and Rob were going to the Academy Awards. I was excited for them and everyone who had worked on the film. ILM also sent the VFX producers and some of the key leads to the Academy Awards as well.

It was an absolute blast to go with my colleagues. The entire evening was nonstop entertainment. It is quite an experience to be part of a live broadcast that was sent out to the rest of the world. A lot more goes on behind the scenes than what an average viewer sees on television. The awards ceremony was held at the Shrine Auditorium near the University of Southern California in Los Angeles. We arrived hours before it started. It was pretty exciting to walk the red carpet. My seat was on the main floor next to one of my colleagues. Right after the show began, Angelina Jolie and her brother walked right in front of us to their seats. She won an Oscar for Supporting Actress in the film *Girl Interrupted* that night. The VFX award was announced early in the show, and it went to *The Matrix*. We were bummed, but very proud to have been nominated for our work.

When I finished Star Wars in the spring of 1999, there was another film called *The Perfect Storm* for which the research and development stage had already begun. An entire team of brilliant technical directors and a physicist were brought in to figure out how to create computer-generated water, for starters. At this point, the research and development portion had been awarded, but not for the entire show yet. I knew the stakes for this one were high. Their mission was focused on getting a fishing boat to move through different types of water from gentle waves to extremely large waves on the ocean. The most difficult and dramatic moment in the script was the shot of the *Andrea Gail* as it climbed up an enormous wave, over 100 feet tall. Nothing like this had ever been attempted, let alone contemplated how it could be done in a film. This was what this team had been grappling with for the past year.

I stopped by Habib's desk; Habib was one of the technical directors working on it before I left on vacation. He showed me some tests of the boat moving through flat calm water. I was so impressed with what they had accomplished so far. Based on my fishing experience in Alaska, I knew the way the boat moved did not look right; it seemed that the weight was not centered correctly.

The salmon fishing season in Alaska was underway, so I contacted my friend Nance in Petersburg about getting some footage of a boat moving through the water, preferably listing to the side about to capsize. I'm not sure which fishermen she asked, but I soon received some great footage that I handed over to Habib and the research and development team for reference.

When I got back from vacation, the studio awarded the show to ILM, and production had already begun with the VFX supervisor, Stefen, and the VFX associate producer, Gretchen. I assumed they would have put an experienced producer on the show, but they picked me. The years I had spent commercial fishing in Alaska had actually primed me for a project like this in ways I could not have imagined or dreamed of. I knew the complexity involved to create realistic water through VFX was enormous—my next adventure had begun.

One of the first things I did when I started on the show was to take Stefen and the key department leads out on an actual boat. It became clear soon after we left the dock from Fisherman's Wharf, exactly how the ocean looked and felt. Lots of reference photos were taken, especially of the bubbles and ripples as they moved across the surface and splashed over the bow and stern. In a nutshell, the visual effects process was to create realistic images like these through digital or computer technology, as an all-CGI shot or added to a live action plate. A core fundamental approach I learned at ILM was the importance of physically experiencing the realism we were going to create in VFX. After we passed under the Golden Gate Bridge into the open ocean it started to get choppy so we headed back. We all got a taste of what it felt like to be on the ocean.

There were plenty of long days and weekends spent on this show for all of us who worked on it. Many lunches and dinners were ordered from a variety of restaurants in the North Bay to keep the energy up toward the end of the show. Often, I made the rounds in the evenings to check in with everyone who had to stay late. Some of us had to work through the Thanksgiving holiday because of one shot. It was the dramatic climax of the film, when the boat climbs up the 100-foot wave, which ended up as the most difficult and most expensive shot in the entire film.

Amazingly, we delivered on time and on budget. Right after the director finalized the last shot, we popped bottles of champagne in the production office with the whole crew to celebrate. I was invited to the premiere. It was quite memorable to go to my first one and see the finished film on the big screen. When the last shot of the film came up with the boat leaving the harbor, there was my name, as a single credit before it went to black. I literally almost fell off my seat in the theater. My credit had always been much later on in the general credit roll and sometimes with the rest of the others under visual effects in alphabetical order at the end of the credits. Many decisions are made on every film regarding where a person's credit goes, but I think it was the director, Wolfgang Petersen's decision, to place it there. I've gotten some really nice credit placement on other films but not as impressive as this one.

At the end of each year, several VFX companies submit their work done in films to the Visual Effects Society. They were reviewed by the members who vote on them and choose ten to be shown at the "bake off" held in Los Angeles. This was the largest social gathering of the year for people in the VFX industry, which I often attended. At the bake off, the VFX supervisor explains the work, then shows the reel and answers questions. It usually goes late into the evening. After the bake off, the members vote for the three nominees for Best Visual Effects at the Academy Awards.

The Perfect Storm was one of the three films selected. We were in a unique situation that year because of the ground-breaking work we did. I do not think many of the people in the Academy who attended the "bake off" had a clear understanding of how we created the CGI water or the amount of shots it was used in. I went to the Oscars with Stefen and the other leads who worked on the film. The excitement for all of us was palpable as we walked down the red carpet to the award's ceremony. As the presenter opened up the envelope, I honestly thought this time Stefen's name would be announced. Instead, it was a sharp jolt when the Oscar for Best Visual Effects went to *Gladiator*. That night they pretty much swept the awards, winning a total of twelve Oscars. The next day film critic Roger Ebert wrote in his column that we were robbed. He must have gone to the bake off.

After we wrapped, I took a well-deserved but short vacation with Nolan. ILM wanted me back soon to take over another project that had already started. The film was *A.I. Artificial Intelligence*, directed by Steven Spielberg. The last time I had worked on one of his films was *Jurassic Park*, when I was a production assistant. It was quite a different experience to work directly with him as the VFX producer. I was so happy to be working with Scott and Dennis again, who were the two VFX supervisors on the show. They both had worked with Steven before and knew the lay of the land.

This show was different from the previous two I had worked on. It involved more organizational skills to balance and prioritize all the moving parts between the practical and visual effects. The bar was raised quite a bit higher on this show. Besides the VFX work, several miniature models were built, as were the builds for practical sets. We had three stages going at the same time. I thoroughly enjoyed the challenge and opportunity to work more on the practical side of production.

Several other things were happening during this same time period—2000 through 2001. Nolan was a senior in high school, figuring out where to attend college. I was so busy on the show that he had to research the universities he was interested in on his own. The top of his list were the schools in California. He wisely chose the University of California at San Diego.

The most difficult and emotional part came at the end of show during the final weeks, which is always stressful by itself. My sweet dear grandad, who was 101 years old, had a small stroke that put him in the hospital for a couple of days. The prognosis was not good. Nolan and I visited him at the hospital. Soon he was taken home to be cared for by Minnie, the family, and hospice care. A hospital bed was set up in one of the guest rooms. I took turns spending the night in the same room to care for him during the night until he passed on that Easter weekend. He had lived a remarkably full life, one that Nolan and I were so grateful to have been a part of. Eight years later, his wife Minnie, passed on in May of 2009 at the age of ninety-nine.

There was a standard practice at ILM on how a show was run. Each one had a weekly production meeting with the supervisor, producer, and the department leads. Those meetings discussed the status of the shots in progress and when they were scheduled to be finished. This was an essential part of keeping the show on track and reaching the end goal, finishing all the work by the final delivery date. Another weekly meeting for me was with the show's accountant. Staying on budget was incredibly important on every show I worked on. At the end of the day, the most important part of my job was taking care of every single person on my crew. I knew they were putting in at least 150 percent of their time and energy into this show. They all deserved a great deal of respect and kindness for what was being achieved on every single shot.

Another important aspect of the job was building a rapport with the director, producers, and the studio, which was not always easy but critical at every juncture of the project. The support I had at ILM was the best. It was a given that your show would deliver on time. Sometimes there were situations when a show needed additional crew to help complete shots and meet the delivery date. Management at ILM was always in the loop, so they knew when and how much to shift crews around. This was never a simple feat by any means, but they always made it work.

A.I. Artificial Intelligence was nominated for Best Visual Effects in March of 2002. This was the third time I went to the Academy Awards. Dennis, Scott, the leads, and I thoroughly enjoyed all the festivities. It was quite an honor to be recognized by the Academy regardless of who won. That year, *The Lord of the Rings: The Fellowship of the Ring* received the Oscar.

The visual effects talent pool continued to expand as new VFX companies cropped up in the United States and other parts of the world. The next group of projects I worked on involved a couple of sequences, not the entire body of VFX work. Sometimes we were brought in when a show did not have enough resources to complete the VFX work on time. We referred to them as 911s. Each one had its unique set of challenges to solve. It was never boring.

By 2002, plans to move the company to the Presidio in San Francisco had been in the works for several years, but now it was taking shape. This meant big changes were about to happen for several of us living in Sonoma County, an hour commute from the city on a good day. I decided to start getting the word out to friends and colleagues in the industry that I might be looking for freelance work in the Los Angeles area in the near future.

From 2002 to 2003, I was put on a film called *Hidalgo*, which involved several months of location work in the US and Morocco. I felt this was the perfect opportunity for me to do this because Nolan was living in San Diego attending his second year of college at UCSD. From my previous experiences, I knew the knowledge and information gained on set was an invaluable resource during post-production. I looked forward to having this opportunity.

The film was a western set in the 1890's, so the type of work we did was very different from the other projects

I had worked on. The challenges ranged in scope from creating an intense desert wind storm to animals such as horses, locusts and leopards. We also did matte paintings, which were designed in the Orientalist style, particularly those done by the artist, Jean-Leon Gerome. They captured the exotic landscapes and cultures of the Middle East and Northern Africa during this time period.

For several months, Tim, the VFX supervisor, Lanny, the 3D match mover, and I were on location. One of the key VFX components on set besides the images from the film camera is getting precise, accurate measurements and distance of the movement occurring in the live action footage. This happened for each VFX shot when we were on set. This information is essential for the VFX team back at the facility.

The shoot began in Montana near Glacier National Park on the Blackfoot Reservation for the last scene in the film with the lead actor, Viggo Mortensen. It was nice to start out with a small cast and crew. The odds of having worked with some of them before or knowing some of the same people happened a lot on-set. One of the conversations I had with Viggo was about that very subject. It turned out, we had both been in Rome at Cinecitta Studios around the same time working on the film *Daylight* eight years ago.

Some of the climatic shots in this scene were filled with hundreds of wild mustang horses as they raced down the hill to freedom. The director wanted the wide shots to be completely full, but the horse trainers could not keep them all together in the frame. To achieve the look Joe wanted, we shot live-action plates of groups as they ran down different sections of the hill. It was tricky to get them to do this, but astonishingly, they did. In post-production, we comped plates together to fill the frame with magnificent wild mustang horses. These shots were intercut with Viggo Mortensen's character, Frank Hopkins, as he unsaddles his beloved horse, Hidalgo, setting him free with the rest of the herd. It was quite a poignant and beautiful end to the story.

The next location was in South Dakota, near the Black Hills and the Pine Ridge Reservation. This was Lakota country. The Lakota were known as the horse nation, where the warrior Crazy Horse, fought valiantly for his people and their traditional way of life. Rightfully so, he became the symbol of resistance against oppressive governments worldwide. I was drawn to the Lakota people, particularly, Crazy Horse, since I was a teenager and knew his story needed to be told. Fast forward thirty years, when I met Sonny, an actor in the film and Lakota medicine man, and his friend Timon. One of the many conversations we had was about my idea to make a feature film about the last part of Crazy Horse's life. Before we moved on to our next location, Sonny gave me his blessing and told me to go for it. This sparked the beginning of my circuitous journey to make the film.

Morocco was next where the majority of the location work was shot. A lot of the filming was done around the city of Erfoud in the southeastern part of the country, near the Algerian border. We had already been on location for several weeks in the United States when Tim, Lanny and I got on the plane in San Francisco for our flight to Morocco. For some reason, I checked all of my luggage except the backpack with my personal things, paperwork, and computer. After a more than sixteen-hour flight with two long layovers, we arrived late in Ouarzazate and were quite exhausted by this point. It was a small airport, and everyone's luggage was there on the carousel except mine.

The clothes I had on were all I had after two days of travel. Tim and Lanny lent me some of their t-shirts, but I had to find proper clothing and a pair of shoes to tide me over until my luggage arrived. The driver assigned to our VFX team, was Ahmed, a Moroccan who spoke perfect English. The next day he took me to one of the markets. They were mostly small shops filled with rows of clothes stacked up to the ceiling, nothing like the stores in the US or Europe. There were no dressing rooms or mirrors, and the sizes were written in Arabic. With Ahmed's help, I eyeballed the pants and tops then bought a couple pairs of each. The shoes were the most difficult to find because I had long narrow feet; the only ones that fit were men's. Thank goodness my luggage showed up three weeks later.

When we had to be on set, Ahmed drove us to the location somewhere out in the Sahara Desert. I usually sat in the front seat with him, which led to many conversations about his culture. He gave me a crash course about their language, told me that the sound I heard each morning around 3 A.M. was the first call to prayer, and explained the proper etiquette for women in this predominately Muslim country. The group of ethnic indigenous people we worked with throughout the shoot were the Berbers. We were often invited into their homes for the traditional midafternoon tea, a lovely way to experience their kind, generous hospitality.

Each time we drove out to the location in the desert, the dunes had shifted and reshaped overnight, depending on the direction and velocity of the wind. This kind of landscape was completely foreign to me. The winds were a daily occurrence, so proper clothing was key to getting through the day. Since I had contacts, it was essential to wear a pair of sunglasses that fit tightly around my eyes to protect them at all times. Another item I wore when we were in the desert was a scarf wrapped around my face to keep the sand out. When we shot exterior plates, it was always with a small crew.

Horses were an essential part of the story, and the climax in the film was the famous "Ocean of Fire" horse race across the desert, which involved the riders going through a severe dust storm. To create this, the tight shots were done practically on set, but the wide shots with the giant wall of sand engulfing them was done in post-production through visual effects. Before we filmed the shots for this scene, the riders warmed up on their horses. They were all experienced equestrians from Spain. It was like watching poetry in motion, as they moved perfectly in sync with the horse. This brought back a lot of fond memories of when I used to show with my horse in three-day events.

Halfway through the shoot in Morocco, Joe, the director, along with the producers, decided to shorten the shoot scheduled for the port city of El Jadida. They chose to send a small crew to shoot the plates for our matte paintings, which meant we were going. Our cross-country adventure with Ahmed began as we left the desert and drove up over the Atlas Mountains to the city of Marrakesh, where we stopped for the night. We explored the open market in the city center and had some delicious kabobs from one of the street vendors. As we walked around, suddenly I felt something climb up my shoulder. It certainly got my attention as this small well-dressed monkey latched onto me. When I turned around, this man just smiled at me and cheerfully picked up the monkey. This was one of several unique experiences I had during my time in Morocco. Another one was when we drove through small villages. I did not wear a hijab over my head, so I would duck down out of sight in respect to one of their religious traditions. The drive across the country further broadened my understanding of the country and their culture.

After we arrived in El Jadida, the contrast from the desert to the cool refreshing breezes coming off the ocean was a welcome change. We filmed in different parts of the city, mainly in the old historical district founded by the Portuguese. One of the locations was near a racetrack where we filmed shots of this beautiful Arabian horse. The trainer kindly let me ride the horse; it was pure joy for me.

When I worked on location, I really enjoyed working with cast and crew from different parts of the world. On this show, most of the crew was from the United States, England, Spain, and Morocco. Frequently, the first assistant director for second unit, Jamie, who was British, would let me know with his lovely cheery accent that we were headed out for a "recce" (pronounced "recky"). I was perplexed at first and had no idea what he meant. I quickly learned it was the British slang word for reconnaissance, which was the same as a location scout. It totally cracked me up when I heard him say that word. I knew it meant Tim and I were about to embark on another adventure.

After we finished the location work, I returned home with Tim and Lanny to start the post-production work at ILM. Some of our shots required additional tight shots with the actor, Omar Sharif. We had met him when we were on location in Morocco. He always came across as a warm, charming person. In the film, he played the character Sheikh Riyadh, who invites Frank to Arabia to compete in the "Ocean of Fire" horse race across the desert. It was such a delight to spend an afternoon with him on one of the stages at ILM. We shot close-ups of him in costume against a blue screen and comped them into background plates. A couple of those shots ended up in the film.

Spending several months in Morocco with those gorgeous Arabian horses on the film sets of *Hidalgo* rejuvenated my interest in riding again. One of the technical directors at ILM who was working on the show, told me about the equestrian center in Santa Rosa where she took lessons and competed in equestrian events with her horse. Since my son was in college at UCSD, I had time on the weekends to take riding lessons at the stables that were conveniently close to Sebastopol. For the next several months, I did dressage, stadium, and cross country jumping, loving every minute. I was a little rusty, but those instincts clicked in. Being one with the horse and flying over those jumps was sheer joy, just as I remembered it.

When the show wrapped in the fall of 2003, I took a trip to Europe to visit Nolan in Budapest, Hungary. He was studying international policy his junior semester at Corvinus University. While I was waiting for my flight at LAX in Los Angeles, Ken's other son, Brian, called to tell me Ken was missing at sea. I was stunned. It had been several years since either one of us had been in touch with him, which made the news even more difficult to wrap my head around. He had left the docks in Coos Bay, Oregon, days before, to fish for tuna. No one heard a mayday or distress signal from him. The boat had vanished. The Coast Guard searched for several days but did not find anything.

During the years I lived and fished with Ken in Alaska, there were commercial fishermen who had been lost at sea and never found. But I never thought Ken would be one of them. He always had a sixth sense when it came to finding the fish and getting out of dangerous situations when we were out on the ocean. I had experienced some of these situations with him, and we had always gotten back safely, but this time, it was not meant to be.

Brian told me he had gone out fishing on his wooden hulled boat, the *C-Lady*, by himself. I knew the boat well because we had both admired the boat with its classic elegant lines, making it seaworthy and ideal for commercial fishing. Old timers called it a skookum boat. I was not surprised he had bought that boat. I decided not to tell Nolan until I saw him in person to explain what had happened to his dad. This was not easy for Nolan to grasp losing a father he did not know very well. One year later, in May of 2005, we attended Ken's memorial in Coos Bay, Oregon, to pay our last respects, finding some closure of his passing.

A lot of changes were happening for me after *Hidalgo* was released in March of 2004. News was already circulating around ILM that they were moving to the Presidio in San Francisco. This meant I would have a much longer commute. Other changes were happening, too. Nolan graduated from college in June from UCSD and decided to teach English to grade school children in Seoul, South Korea, for a year.

It felt like the right time to make a major change and leave ILM. It was not an easy decision to make after spending fifteen years of my career with this company. It was a remarkable period in my life, and I was going to deeply miss the extraordinary, talented people at ILM. However, I was ready to venture out and explore new adventures.

Once the word got out I was leaving, the head of visual effects at Disney Studios interviewed me for a VFX Producer position on the film *Eight Below*. I got the job. The next chapter had begun.

Shifting Gears

In January of 2005, I went to Los Angeles to start work on the film. Arrangements were made with a friend from church to stay at my condo in Sebastopol. Amy, who I had worked with on *Meet Joe Black*, had a spare bedroom ready for me. Once pre-production began, it took a short period of time to get established in my new role. Fortunately, I had worked with Frank, the director and producer, before on *The Indian in the Cupboard* when I was a VFX coordinator.

Work as a freelance VFX producer involved other responsibilities than what I had at ILM but were very similar.

A significant part of my job was keeping the studio updated on a daily basis, since I was their eyes and ears on the production. Also, having a sixth sense was a crucial part of it, which allowed me to stay on top of information pertaining to VFX, and assess who, when, and how much of it was relevant to staying on track, on budget, and on schedule. While it was pretty straightforward in theory, in some ways it was more challenging because now I was the conduit between the director, editor, studio, and VFX facilities.

Our first location was on a picturesque mountain outside the town of Smithers in northern British Columbia, Canada. We shot the exterior scenes there between January and March with the sled dogs and the lead actors. The majority of the filming was done in freezing cold conditions, making it imperative to have layers of proper winter gear keeping you as warm as possible. This included a tuque, which is was what the Canadians call a warm, knitted stocking hat. Smithers was known for world-class skiing, so there were plenty of places to purchase gear from ski shops around town.

The heads of departments on the show were all assigned an SUV during the shoot. This included me. Often, I drove to the location by myself, but sometimes, Char, the data technician and her dog, Jake, rode with me. Usually a mix of rock and roll songs, especially U2, played, energizing us for another adventurous day up on the mountain.

After arriving at base camp and dropping my things off at the production office, I climbed aboard the all-terrain Hagglunds. The vehicle took us straight up the mountain, over the snowcapped terrain to where we were shooting that day. It was quite a ride. No matter where I sat, we all slid to the opposite end, just depended on whether the vehicle was traveling up or down the mountain. It was absolutely hilarious watching everyone cling to the bench, trying to hold on. The other mode of transportation was a snowmobile, which was a lot more fun and guaranteed exceptional views of the entire mountain range and the valley below. When the exterior shots were completed, the cast and crew flew to Vancouver, Canada, to film interior scenes at one of the studios in town.

Being on location was a unique experience. It meant spending lots of time with the cast and crew, forming a special bond with them. I really enjoyed that part, especially with the VFX team, Char, and Andre. The difficult aspect of it were long periods of time spent away from family and friends. I was so happy Nolan was able to visit when I was in Vancouver and go on set, giving him a clearer sense of what my job entailed now.

After we wrapped principal photography, I went back to LA for post-production, finishing up the VFX work at the end of 2005. I had an interview for another possible job, but it did not pan out. Actually, I was relieved to have some time off. During post-production, a colleague, Steve, and his wife Helen, let me stay at the bungalow they were renting in Santa Monica. Through them I got to know the landlord, who told me another one two doors down would be available soon.

Now my plans to relocate were in full swing. A couple of months later I sold my condo in lovely Sebastopol where my son and I had lived for seventeen years. I left behind so many incredible memories: watching my son Nolan grow up, being an integral part of Grandad and Minnie's life, and the close friendships we made had been a significant, remarkable time in our lives and would always hold a special place in our hearts.

Being based in Santa Monica was an ideal location for me, close to my dear friends, Erika and Richard, who lived in the Pacific Palisades and seven blocks from the beach where I took my early morning walks. It was a half a block off of Montana Avenue, close to a variety of shops, coffee houses, and the Aero Theater, which showed foreign and independent films, and brought in guest directors to discuss their work. One of the guests was the talented French director Agnes Varda. After her talk, a group of us joined her for a glass of wine across the street. This part of LA definitely suited me, even though living on the west side guaranteed a long commute to the film studios in the valley.

I continued to look for VFX work and did more research on the Lakota warrior Crazy Horse. This led me in a different direction for the storyline, away from the romanticized version of Mari Sandoz's *Crazy Horse: The Strange Man of the Oglalas*. It drew me to his resistance against the United States government and standing up for his people.

I mentioned this idea to my cousin John, a well known Nebraska historian, which opened up several discussions about this mysterious man of the Lakota. This got the ball rolling. I started piecing together a rough outline for a feature film focused on this pivotal juncture in his life and the Lakota, abruptly altering their way of life forever. During this tumultuous period, these events led to his untimely tragic death at Camp Robinson, in western Nebraska, on September 5, 1877. This was the part of the story that needed to be told.

In the spring of 2006, I still had no work, so I decided to do some traveling. My first trip was to visit Nolan in Seoul, South Korea, where he was spending the year teaching English to grade school children. Then I continued on to Kyoto, Japan, to meet up with Mandy and Jim's family. To have the time and resources to visit this part of the world for the first time was pretty remarkable. After I got back to Santa Monica, there were a couple of leads for a job, but nothing panned out. My next trip was to Europe and the

Cannes Film Festival in mid-May. I really enjoyed meeting other producers and filmmakers as well as attending some film premieres at the festival.

When I returned home, work on the Crazy Horse project continued while I looked for VFX work. I also wrote about my experiences in Alaska when I commercial fished with Ken. Even though Nolan had heard most of the stories, it was important to write them down, painting a broader picture of that lifestyle and the town of Sitka, where he was born.

I had kept in touch with Timon, who had accompanied Sonny, the Lakota Medicine Man, during the filming of *Hidalgo* in 2003 when he had given me his blessing to pursue a film about Crazy Horse. This was the beginning of my journey to make a film about him. More research, discussions, and outlines transpired over the next several years. Eventually, Timon wrote the script for a feature film based on the last year of Crazy Horse's life. I optioned it in May of 2012 for three years. When the film project got to this point, the wheels were turning. A year after that, I would face a dramatic event altering my career and life forever.

Halfway Across the World

In the spring of 2007, during the development of Crazy Horse and my other projects, I was fortunate to get some VFX producing jobs. The next one was *The Mummy: Tomb of the Dragon Emperor*, directed by Rob Cohen. Years earlier, he had directed the film *Daylight* that was shot at Cinecitta Studios outside of Rome, Italy. On that show, I was the VFX coordinator and went on location for the first time with the team from ILM. I was looking forward to working with him again, this time as the VFX producer.

The show had a lot of VFX, including some really challenging work. The first two films of this very popular trilogy were set in the middle East, shot in Morocco, near some of the locations where we filmed *Hidalgo*. For the third installment, several major changes were made. The story takes place years later in 1946, when the famous couple's son, Alex, makes a significant archaeological find in a remote part of China. The stakes seemed to be higher on this one, ratcheting up the level of complexity to tell the story, including the VFX work.

The VFX work was mainly focused on creating the ruthless Dragon Emperor and his mighty army of terra cotta warriors that had been buried in clay for a millennium. One of the big challenges was bringing them back to life in the same time period as the film, which is set in 1946. This creates all kinds of havoc throughout the film, which translates into lots of VFX work and was no small feat to manage. Thank goodness the studio added another VFX producer, Garv, and our coordinator, Paula soon after I started. We also brought on talented VFX facilities and their teams early on to accomplish all of the challenging work required on this film.

Soon after I left ILM in 2005, my personal email address was added to one of the Yahoo groups with other colleagues who had left, as a way to keep in touch. Quite a few of us refer to it as "the collective brain trust." I relied on it a lot, often posting questions for complicated VFX problems that came up on set. There was always a quick response with an answer. I was grateful to have this connection.

This was also where colleagues found out about my accident and the link to the Caring Bridge page Nolan had set up to keep everyone informed on my condition. When I was able to read emails, several popped up with words of encouragement. Months into my recovery, I was able to compose a short note to the group, thanking them for their incredible support. The simple act of reconnecting with them at this point helped me remember with more clarity who I was before the accident happened.

Our first location on the film was in Montreal, Canada, during the summer months of 2007, in the heart of Quebec. It was nice being in the midst of French culture again. I scoped out the restaurants near my apartment in the old part of the city and found one that served a dish I discovered in Cannes, France, a year earlier. It was *soupe de poisson*, a soup made with fish stock, with melted cheese over the broth and chunks of a toasted baguette on top—yum. I frequented this place several times during my stay in the city.

The summer was filled with festivals and outdoor concerts throughout the city. Right after we arrived, we were still in pre-production before we started principal photography, giving most of us time to enjoy some of the festivities. A group of us went to one of the Just for Laughs comedy shows, a slice of Québécois dry, subtle humor. It was an absolutely hilarious evening. And I enjoyed a couple of amazing free outdoor concerts, too.

My morning commute to Mel's Cite du Cinema Studios took me across a bridge past the island where the 1967 World's Fair, Expo 67, took place. I had been there with my family when I was eleven years old. Seeing it again after all those years brought back vivid memories, particularly the international exhibits and Habitat '67, the modern housing structure that was still there on the island. This experience widened my understanding of the world, sparking a curiosity and desire to explore those places and their cultures.

At the studio, we shot interior scenes, replicating the site in Xian, China, where the Terra Cotta army was found. The studio's model shop made hundreds of exact replicas out of fiberglass, lightweight and easy to move around for each setup. We added hundreds more VFX terra cotta warriors in the wide shots to fill up the background during post-production.

The remaining locations took us halfway across the world to China. I had one day at home in Santa Monica before the thirteen-hour flight to Beijing, arriving the next morning around 5 A.M., to the city where we were based for a couple of weeks. Exhausted from the long trip, I decided to stay up for the day and orient myself to the new time zone. Later that morning, I joined some of the crew on a sightseeing trip to the Great Wall, giving me a memorable introduction to this fascinating country.

The next location was in the Tianmo Desert in Hebei Provence of northwestern China. Around this area, we shot exteriors for the scenes of General Yang's camp in Ming Village and when the terra cotta warriors awaken, led by the Dragon Emperor, played by Jet Li. The commute was a good hour from where we were staying, so we had to leave early in the morning before sunrise. The first morning, I noticed a large group of people in the parking lot below, quietly moving in sync with each other. I was perplexed and curious.

On our long drive to the location, I described this to our driver. He smiled, explaining that this was a common practice usually done first thing in the morning throughout China. It was tai chi, which began centuries ago as a form of martial arts. Over time, it has developed into an exercise focused on fluid, graceful movements and meditation, practiced all over the world.

The drive back to our apartments at the end of the day had its own little adventures. The Chinese producers on the show had hired a crew they placed at specific locations along the route back to where we were staying. When the crew saw us stuck in traffic, they stopped the other long line of vehicles, mainly trucks, to let us through. After we wrapped for the day at that location, the driver often took us back a different route. A couple of times we went on country roads instead on paved highways. Those roads had enormous potholes that went through what appeared to be small impoverished villages, giving us a very different view of China.

In the summer of 2007, after a long flight, arriving in the wee hours of the morning, I unpacked my suitcases and joined several of the crew on *The Mummy: Tomb of the Dragon Emperor*, to explore part of the Great Wall of China.

We spent a couple of weeks in northwestern China shooting VFX plates in the desert for the scene with the terra cotta army, Ming Guo and his men. Through VFX, they came alive and rose out of the sand, causing all kinds of havoc, led by the Dragon Emperor played by Jet Li.

One of the weekends we had off, a couple of us went into Beijing to do some sightseeing. I went with Paula and another VFX coordinator who had grown up there. She took us on a tour around the city. The first stop was Tiananmen Square, in the city center, one of the main tourist attractions. Walking around the square, it seemed pristine and orderly. There was no indication or historical marker regarding the June, 1989 pro-democracy student demonstration. This event had erupted into a violent confrontation with the army, killing several protesters. It felt like the government had just wiped it away, leaving an eerie sense of calm.

Then we went to the Forbidden City and on to the most interesting part of the tour for me, the Caochangdi Art District. We visited several galleries and artists' studios, which gave me a sense of contemporary Chinese art. We also saw Ai Weiwei's, studio house, which he designed. It was brilliant. The next stop was the oldest pharmacy in the city, known for its healing medicinal herbs. The last place we went to was an incredible silk store where I bought a lovely silk scarf and robe for my mom.

When we finished shooting at that location, we flew to Shanghai to work at the studio outside the city. Our VFX team spent the rest of the shoot there, filming the interior and exterior scenes, including Rick's nightclub. Rob, the director, used some of the crew as extras in the dance scene at the club. I am in a couple of those shots, elegantly dressed by the talented costume designer, Sanja.

After we wrapped in China, the VFX team went back to Los Angeles for several months of post-production work. When I arrived home, there was a large wooden box sitting on the patio in front of the bungalow with my name written on it. True to his word, Bruce, the special effects coordinator, had shipped one of the fiberglass life-size terra cotta warriors with his gear back to Los Angeles. It was so kind and thoughtful that he did this for me. Since then, it has stood quietly in the corner wherever I am living, keeping watch over my humble abode.

A lot of great VFX work was done on this film that everyone was proud of, finishing on time and on budget. *The Mummy: Tomb of the Dragon Emperor* was released on August 1, 2008.

After the show wrapped, I went back to Nebraska to visit family and friends. For some reason, Mom had not gotten the package I sent her with the robe and scarf. When I got to her house and checked the stack of mail in the entry way, it was there, buried in the middle of the pile. I thought she had been too busy and did not remember getting it. Eventually, more situations like this occurred. I did not realize it than, but these were early signs of her dementia.

After I got back to Santa Monica, a colleague of mine, Richard, who I had worked with on *Eight Below*, contacted me regarding a film project he wanted me to help him develop. I was delighted to, along with Marjo, another producer I had worked with at ILM. Over the next couple of months, we lined up meetings with prospective investors, which included a trip to the Dubai Film Festival in the United Arab Emirates in December of 2008.

Our focus at the festival was to find financial backing for the film. We met other producers and filmmakers pitching their own projects, too. The city of Dubai is located on the Persian Gulf, a central hub for oil in the Middle East. There are several modern high rise skyscrapers that dot the skyline. A famous one was the iconic sail-shaped Buri Al Arab Jumeriah luxury hotel with a bar and restaurant on the top floor with spectacular views. We met some colleagues there for cocktails. Outside the city, man-made islands were built on the gulf with well-designed neighborhoods. For my first visit to the Middle East, I was quite impressed with the culture and their sophisticated style of architecture.

Back in Santa Monica, I continued to do some work on Richard's project, but nothing panned out from our trip to Dubai. I continued to do more work on the Crazy Horse project, too. In May of 2009, at the age of ninety-nine, dear, sweet Minnie passed on at her home in Sebastopol, California. A couple of weeks later, my friend, Riz started work on the film *The Other Guys* with Pat, one of the producers. They knew I was available, which led to an interview with the head of VFX, Lori, at Sony Studios. They hired me for the job.

This time the location was in New York City for the duration of pre-production and principal photography starting that summer through December of 2009. Production lined up an apartment for me in the same building as Riz on 26th Street and 6th Avenue in Manhattan. It was an easy, quick commute on the #1 or #2 trains to the production office.

I had a lot of visitors, including Nolan, and friends Jim, Mandy, and her sister, Katie. We had a great time exploring the city together. Soon after I got settled in, I found out my friend Julie was living in NYC with her husband, George. We were roommates in college and had kept in touch off and on over the years. We met up several times, rekindling our wonderful friendship. The city was filled with a treasure trove of fascinating things to do. I went to concerts, museums, Broadway shows, art galleries, and some amazing restaurants with friends and colleagues. This was when I pretty much fell in love with New York City.

The director of the film, Adam McKay, and one of the lead actors, Will Ferrell, had worked together since their days at Saturday Night Live. His style of directing was more collaborative than some of the previous directors I had worked with, bringing department leads into the conversation early on during pre-production. This kind of interaction is always important, especially since it was his first film using visual effects. In some ways, it was a learning curve for all of us, keeping everyone on the same page in terms of what was required of us and how to achieve the end result for what Adam wanted in the film.

This was essential for scenes like the one at Chelsea Piers when the helicopter flies into the driving range and crashes. It was simple on paper, but several things were involved to pull it off in the final shot. Another one was the scene at the bar when Will's and Mark's characters appear to be in different places as the camera glides through the bar. The camera dolly move was repeated several times and blended together through VFX in post-production.

The amount of VFX work on this show was more manageable and straightforward. We had a great team with Gregor, the VFX supervisor who I had worked with at ILM and Viet, the coordinator. The lead VFX facility team, Jim and Cara, were based in NYC and did an incredible job along with the other VFX companies who worked on the show.

After we finished filming all the principal photography in December, I went to Vienna, Austria, where Nolan had an internship. It was great to spend Christmas with him and enjoy their festive traditions. The streets were filled with beautifully lit decorations, and the outdoor Christmas markets had an array of delicious holiday foods, making this holiday a memorable one. Then I flew back to Santa Monica to start post production in January, finishing up with the VFX work in the spring. *The Other Guys* was released in August of 2010.

Around this time, my mom's dementia had progressed quite a bit. It was incredibly heartbreaking to watch her go through this. My brothers and I made the painful decision to move her from Mark's place into Parsons House, an assisted living and memory care facility in Omaha, Nebraska. I often called to visit with her on the phone until she was unable to. It was a very emotional time for all of us.

Things came together quickly on another job in NYC. A colleague I had worked with on *AI: Artificial Intelligence* was based there, doing VFX supervising work. That summer, he was hired to work on the film *Tower Heist* and asked me to join him. The timing for me was perfect. I said "yes."

I returned to NYC that summer in 2010 to start work on the film and had a friend stay at my bungalow in Santa Monica until my lease was up in December. I had made arrangements to stay with my friend, Leah Anne in Long Island City, Queens. It was a convenient location, great neighborhood and a block from the #7 train, an easy commute to the production office on the lower west side of Manhattan.

There were lots of familiar faces on the crew who I had worked with on *The Other Guys*. There was a fair amount of VFX work with its own share of challenges on this film. The VFX team on this one was Mark, Jessica, Bryan, and me along with talented NYC facilities. I was content being back in New York City again.

A couple of weeks after we started pre-production, my dad had some complications from a fall and ended up in the hospital. Things got worse, so I quickly made arrangements to fly back to Omaha, but my flight was delayed until the next morning due to a severe storm. During the night, I texted with Angel, who was with him in the hospital. Late that night, my dear, sweet dad, passed away on September 27, 2010. I was numb. When I got to Omaha early that morning, we started to make plans for the funeral service. My family, cousins, friends, and work associates were there to honor Dad and pay our last respects.

I returned a week later and jumped right into the fray on the first day of shooting. This was the part of principal photography that usually involved the entire crew and several of the actors, depending on what pages in the script were scheduled to be filmed that day. The first week was always hectic. It was not an easy situation for me, but it was probably helpful to be fully immersed with work.

In the midst of this, I was surrounded by the vibrant, boundless energy of New York City. And I was part of a larger circle of friends and colleagues through Leigh Ann, Kristie, Julie, and George, exploring the art and music scene. Two of the organizations I got involved with were the Witness Project based in Guyana, founded by Margaret Clemons, and the International Arts Movement (IAM), founded by the artist, Makoto Fujimura. I often helped out and attended several of the events sponsored by these organizations.

It was clear to me at this point that I wanted to be based in New York City. In November, I found a nice apartment on Vernon Boulevard in Long Island City and moved all my things from Santa Monica when the lease was up in December. My apartment was a couple of blocks from one of the subway stops for the #7 train. It was one stop from Grand Central Station, making the commute to work incredibly convenient. Close by were organic grocery stores, great restaurants, and a lovely park along the East River where I took my morning walk, enjoying the spectacular view of Manhattan. Construction on the new One World Trade Center had just started, so on my walks I could see that magnificent building take shape along the NYC skyline. As in Greek mythology, the phoenix was rising from the ashes, nine years after 9/11.

Throughout the shoot, plenty of interesting situations came up. One in particular was the scene in the penthouse luxury apartment of Alan Alda's character in Trump International Hotel and Tower next to Columbus Circle in midtown. In this particular scene, Ben Stiller's character, along with Eddie Murphy, Casey Affleck, Michael Pina, and Matthew Broderick attempt to steal the car parked in the living room of his apartment that he claimed was the actor, Steve McQueen's 1963 Ferrari 250 GT Lusso race car.

A couple of the exterior shots we had to get for that scene involved putting Mark, our VFX supervisor, on a piece of scaffolding with the film camera, hanging on the side of the building, sixty-three floors up, outside the penthouse. I held my breath, as the wind buffeted the scaffolding back and forth, but he got all of the shots we needed. Another setup we filmed was when the getaway car flips over on the Columbus Circle roundabout causing all kinds of chaos. From the look on the faces of some of the bystanders, it was clear they thought it was a real accident, not staged. My friends Julie and George stopped by while we were filming this, impressed as well, on their way to their violin shop. The stunt team definitely succeeded in making it look real and did it in one take.

Most of the interior scenes like the swimming pool looking out over Manhattan were shot on the stages at the Brooklyn Navy Yard. Growing up, I often heard stories about this place from Dad when he was stationed there during WWII. To be physically in the same place brought a sense of nostalgia, wondering what it was like when he was there.

After we finished shooting the film, post-production started with the VFX facilities being awarded the work. All of them were located in NYC relatively close to our VFX office. A couple months later, toward the end of post-production, another family tragedy occurred. My dear sweet mother passed away on October 5, 2011, almost exactly a year after Dad. I flew back to Nebraska the next day to be with my family and make arrangements for the funeral. Our family gathered together with cousins, friends, and associates to pay our last respects, honoring Mom.

After I got back to NYC, I discussed leaving the show with Mark and the studio. They completely understood my situation. I needed to take some time off to grieve the loss of my parents. I handed things over to one of the studio VFX producers and left the show.

A couple of weeks later, I went to Europe. It felt like a fitting tribute to Mom and Dad since they were instrumental in letting me go the first time with a group from high school that inspired my passion for travel. More importantly, I wanted to see my son, who was working in Budapest, Hungary. The first stop was Paris, to visit my dear friend Iris, then onto Rome to meet up with Nolan. These were the two cities I dearly loved, and I visited my favorite Catholic churches and the Sistine Chapel to pray, meditate, and light a candle for Mom and Dad.

When I got back to NYC, I had a couple of interviews for VFX work but nothing panned out, so I started focusing full time on the Crazy Horse project while Timon worked on the script, finishing it in the spring of 2012. I optioned the script and launched into the creative producing role. The next chapter had begun.

Making the Leap to Creative Producer

Over the next couple of months, I discussed a move back to Nebraska with my brother, Mark, to develop the film. He had an extra room in his house where I could stay and plenty of storage room in the basement. Everything was set in motion. I flew back the middle of October, 2012 to officially begin development on the film. I started a production company, Platte River Pictures, happy and content, launching into making a film about the Lakota warrior, Crazy Horse. Another producer, Mike, and the line producer, Payton, came on board to work with me, putting together a budget and a shooting schedule. This was the first big step followed by putting together a polished proposal with my friend Chuck. This would be used for presentations to raise the funds for getting the film made.

While I settled in, Mark's son, Joey, moved back from California, while he was in between jobs, so it was a full house. His daughter, Angel, and her husband Matt lived about five minutes away with their beautiful daughter, Aviana, who was fourteen months old. My other brother, John, and Robin were not too far away in Norfolk, Nebraska, along with his two sons, John Richard and Andrew. I was really happy to be near my family again.

The day after we celebrated Thanksgiving, Mark got a call from Angel. I could tell by the look on his face, something was seriously wrong. That morning, their precious daughter, Aviana, had not woken up. Matt tried resuscitating her, but she did not respond. The shock and sorrow reverberated throughout our families and friends as we mourned her passing.

The following year, starting in February of 2013, I made several trips to Chadron, Nebraska in the Panhandle, to meet with Bamm, the organizer for the Crazy Horse Ride, to discuss making a documentary about the event. I let him know that I was in the very early stages of development on a film about him, which included a scene of this present-day ride. After a couple of meetings, he agreed to it as long as I agreed to his list of things that were off limits including the spiritual ceremonies. The next month, I organized the shoot and hired a crew to film the event in June of 2013.

The ride began at Fort Robinson, Nebraska where Crazy Horse was killed. From there, they rode out on horseback, in honor of him. Over the next four days, we shot lots of great footage of the riders. Crazy Horse's riderless horse following them through the main street of Chadron, cheered on as they went to the county fairgrounds to camp for the first night. The next morning, they continued along Highway 20, eventually going cross country to the Flying Heart Ranch. They camped there for two days, participating in traditional dancing and music. After dinner, at dusk, people, along with some of the elders, sat around camp fires, telling stories late into the evening.

Since the start of the Homestead Act in 1890, this ranch has been owned by the Kadlecek family. The history of this place has significant meaning for the Lakota and Crazy Horse. The camping site is along the creek that was one of Crazy Horse's favorite places, and legend has it, his family brought his body here and placed it up on the hill across from the creek. The book is about his last days told to them by the Lakota elders called *To Kill an Eagle*. It was written by Dave's parents, Mabell and Edward Kadlecek.

All of us on the crew, Timon, Paul, Brian and myself, decided to pitch our tents up on this knoll looking out over the campsite next to the barbed wire fence, except for Princella, the associate producer, who wisely chose to sleep in the car. All the horses on the ride had been unsaddled and were kept in the fenced in area with the campers. In the middle of the night, I was awakened by a loud thundering sound. We all got out of our tents to figure out what was going on. We discovered a group of about ten horses had just raced past our tents on this narrow path and broken through the fence into an expansive, wide open pasture on the other side. It was a moonlit night, so we could see the horses, kicking up their hind legs in a full gallop, gleefully running in the opposite direction from the campgrounds.

Early the next morning, they were corralled and brought back, and the fence was repaired. That was when we saw how close those horses had been to our tents, just missing us. The ride continued cross country to the highway into Pine Ridge, South Dakota, ending at the fairgrounds with the start of the All-Veterans Pow Wow. It was quite an amazing experience, and we definitely captured the essence of the ride honoring Crazy Horse.

The rest of the summer was equally as busy, organizing all the footage we just shot on the Crazy Horse Ride and working with Witness Project youth in Guyana on the script for their short film, *Rebecca's Story*. In August, I went to New York City to meet with the team and traveled with Margaret, Morgan and Rainy to Guyana for the month to give a film workshop to the Witness Project youth, helping them polish the script, how to the use the lights, camera, sound equipment, and cast the actors, direct, and produce a short film. They were focused and quickly learned how to make a powerful film with a simple clear message: the cycle of physical, sexual, and emotional abuse going on in their country needs to come to an end. They were amazed and happy with the results. The film won awards at a couple of film festivals and inspired this group of teenagers to continue on their mission.

After I got back to Omaha, I needed to take a couple of days off before getting back to work on the Crazy Horse projects. This time of the year the weather was typically a bit brisk but sunny and warm, perfect for horseback riding. There was a Benedictine Abby outside of Elkhorn, Nebraska, called Mt. Michael where my brothers went to high school, so I knew the monks who lived there. One of them, Brother Mel, took care of their horses and had invited me to go riding, so we decided to go that Thursday, September 12, 2013. I was excited and really looking forward to taking a nice leisurely ride on the picturesque grounds of Mt. Michael. Minutes after we saddled up the horses and left the paddock . . . BOOM, everything went dark.

5

Full Circle

The sole reason I moved back to Nebraska in the fall of 2012 was to develop and produce the script for a feature film about the Lakota warrior, Crazy Horse. I had just optioned it for three years and was happy to be at this point in my career. I was ready to make the transition from visual effects to the creative producing side. Falling off a horse was not part of the plan. The day after the accident was the beginning of a long, arduous journey of recovery. No one could predict exactly what lay ahead when I came out of the coma a couple weeks later.

The odds of making a full recovery from a traumatic brain injury vary depending on the severity of the injury combined with what part of the brain was affected. Age and physical condition also play a part in it. One thing in my favor was being in shape physically. But not my age, because I was fifty-seven years old when the accident happened. The doctors at Creighton Hospital told my son they were doubtful I would completely recover.

I guess I keep surprising a lot of people because I have fully recovered. It has been a long road that required a lot of patience, love, and support from my family and friends, as well as all the talented doctors, nurses, therapists, and anyone else at the Creighton Hospital and Madonna Rehabilitation Hospital, who have helped to get me through it. I will be forever grateful to all of them for their unwavering kindness and generosity, rooting me on through this particularly challenging time.

The whole experience has profoundly altered my life in ways that are still unfolding. Before the accident, my mode of operation was usually moving at warp speed, especially since the development stage on the film project had just started. There was not even a remote possibility I could return to that level during the first two years of my recovery. So began the journey of figuring out how to get back to the person I was before the accident.

Recognizing the basic ebb and flow of everyday life was difficult to grasp, and I felt disjointed. I was acutely aware of it, but struggled to consciously orient myself back into that life I remembered. As things began to slowly open up and my brain functions improved, I consciously grappled with this new but familiar reality, realizing I had been out of sync with current events and shifts in relationships that had changed for a multitude of reasons. The sheer challenge of piecing it all together was not possible. It was important for people around me to know why.

Looking back, I see it is astounding how many things have changed since the accident. One in particular, is the basic form of communication with another person. Rarely do people simply talk on the phone. Instead, it is the use of an array of options and a variety of devices including smart phones. My texting has improved but sometimes the message gets misconstrued, often resulting in some hilarious misunderstandings. I still prefer a conversation on the phone with one person.

Relearning all these skills and my vocabulary improving during the second year of my recovery, I began to keep a journal. I was starting to connect more dots together with fluidity, expressing my thoughts and feelings coherently. This was how I was attempting to make sense of the perplexing situation I was in. Eventually, I realized writing it down from my perspective may help my family and others who are going through a similar situation have a better understanding of what it was like. This also became a significant, important part of the healing process for me.

When I finished writing this during the summer of 2017, I had no intention of writing anything more. But my therapist saw remarkable improvements across the board: in my vocabulary, thought process, new ideas sprouting up, and fleshing out more memories throughout my life. Writing the experience down also helped me get through some of the PTSD that was surfacing. My initial response to her was "No," I did not want to write more. There were a couple of reasons why, but the main one was the double vision, which kept getting worse with no way to solve it yet. After everything I had been through since the accident, this was the one problem I struggled with the most. And I was emotionally spent at that point.

But later that year in November, the pipeline embolization device procedure was done, stopping the pseudoaneurysm in my brain from getting larger. The results were remarkable. It shrank the pseudoaneurysm, allowing the sixth cranial nerves to function again. One significant result was some movement of the pupil in my left eye closer to the center. I was so relieved and grateful for these results. This inspired me to start writing again, beginning with my childhood, in chronological order. When I started, it felt like the flood gates had been opened up, unearthing a treasure trove of memories that had been dormant since the accident.

Now I knew that because several other parts of my brain were still intact, it was off to the races.

Writing this book also gave me a sense of purpose, rebuilding confidence and revitalizing my passion for storytelling. Before the accident, rarely would I have taken the time to write, let alone about my own life. No doubt my therapist was fully aware of how beneficial this exercise would be in a myriad of ways. The memories were more vivid and connected events together, with more clarity of what had shaped who I was before the accident and who I am today. It also filled in some of the missing gaps in between. This was another unexpected result from the accident.

Hopefully, the surgery in December of 2018 to tighten up one of the muscles in my left eye will be the last one for a long time. With some physical and vision therapy, my balance has improved and helped reorient my brain to function without peripheral vision on the left side. After three years, it is amazing to be at this juncture in my overall recovery. I am incredibly grateful and blessed.

Three months after the eye surgery in March of 2019, I took a trip to New York City and Europe to visit my friends and son as well as to test out the vision impairment. The last time I was in Europe was three years ago and my first trip abroad since the accident when the double vision had started to get worse. I knew full well that not having peripheral vision on the left side would make the experience quite different, but it was more than I anticipated.

The seemingly simple task of maneuvering through large crowds of people as I walked along sidewalks was the first big hurdle. I have learned to stay on one side as much as possible. But it is difficult to do this when there are a lot of people rushing by. Also, it was virtually impossible for people around me to notice my vision impairment unless I said something about it. Crossing the street is quite different as well. If I am by myself, I wait for the green crosswalk signal, then turn my torso to look both ways before I cross, just to make sure. I rely a lot more on my hearing than I did before, but it is always easier, safer, and faster if I go with someone crossing an intersection.

There was only one scary incident in Paris, while Nolan and I crossed the street at the green light. Out of nowhere, an electric scooter narrowly squeezed between us, running a red light, causing the rider to lose his balance, hitting the pavement. We just stood there stunned, watching him jump back on and zip away down the street. Sheer craziness; I was just relieved no one was hurt. There were plenty of other situations like this that we saw in Paris. After I got back to Omaha in April, the city had just allowed riding scooters for a six-month trial period to be used on the streets only, but they were on the sidewalks and hiking paths, causing similar accidents. Hopefully, the city does something about this.

During my trip to New York City and Europe, I realized how much of my identity had been wrapped up in the vision I had before the accident. It had been an intrinsic, integral part of everything I held dear in my life, including being a film producer. Now I understood. It had been a key part of my ability to quickly assess and evaluate situations going on around me, helping me be more aware of what was happening. This was my general mode of operation whether it was outside of work, on a film set, or at a visual effects facility. It had been and still is a defining part of who I was and am as a person.

One of the things that has changed for me over the last seven years is that I no longer have a desire to return to the fast-paced, high-pressured life I had before. I am perfectly content now to live a simpler, low-key life. Even though I still have a tendency to push past my comfort zone, I now have a keen awareness of what my limitations are, and I respect them. I move at a slower pace and am more cautious in general, but not as tentative as I was in the beginning of the recovery.

Finishing this book has also brought me closure to this episode in my life. For the first time since the accident, I no longer feel constrained by the injuries, but a sense of freedom to begin the next chapter in my life. I am not sure exactly what that will be, but at the top of the list is to travel abroad. I usually have a clearer perspective when I travel, and it will give me time to reflect and gather my thoughts about the future.

I sincerely hope this story has given my lovely family and friends a glimpse into the journey I have been on these last seven years. And if this book can provide some encouragement to others going through a similar situation, I will have achieved a great deal more than I thought possible.

Ginger's List of Words

Words written in chronological order starting with the word "tajine." I started this list in the fall of 2014 in the note section of my iPhone, studying the word until I had it memorized.

Closure	Fuchsia
Lens and frames	Archives
Refills	Electric scooter
Ciao	Stacked haircut
Culinary	Vision impairment
Skookum	Drain for the sink
Downpour	Matrix
Equanimity	Zsolnay porcelain factory in Pecs
Columbine	Unevenly
Shooting star	Padlock

Portuguese:	Crispy
Uma bica (coffee)	Delphiniums
Obrigada (thank you)	Ramp to the dock
Por favor (please)	Red crossbill bird
Pastel de nata (pastry)	Megalodon—shark tooth fossil from John Nance's neighbor
Retrain	Dock attached is a piling
Etceteras	Buoy and marker
Cylinder	Jasmine
Candid	Almond extract
Medial rectus recession	Bird of paradise
Hummelsheim	Gardenia
Rejuvenate	Nobel Peace Prize
Convertible	Cast-iron skillet
Cylinders	Easter lilies
Vehicle	Bay leaf
Abalone	Arrowhead from Jasper
Stare	Stormtrooper
Cuisine	Squashed
Submarine—*K19*	Horizontal and vertical

Granite counter tops	Residency
Fragile	Memoir
Portrait	Garage
Maya Angelo	Film critic
Push cart for golf clubs	Critical thinking
Iridescent	Macchiato is espresso w/ foamed milk
Abalone	Baguette
Pipeline Embolization	*Carnitas*—pork in Spanish
Filter	Tape measure
Monologue	Statue
Esoteric	French press
Coils of titanium	Fellowship
Pseudoaneurysm	Lyrics
Progress	Coleus flowers
CDs	Dahlias flowers
Foundry	Hydrate
Regenerate	Dogma
Chanting	Peripheral vision
Discourse	Simultaneous

Alfalfa used as hay for horses and cows	Exhibition
Geology	Geranium
Juicer	Caterpillars
Perfidy	Milkweed-monarch butterflies
Casserole	Morel mushrooms
Influential	Garden trowel
Vespa	Spanish steps
Delicious	Pronounces
The Constitution	Sea lions
Netherlands or Holland and Dutch is the language	Sea otter
Portrait & portraiture	Pink Flamingo
In-N-Out Burger	Sumac
Velociraptor	Prime rib
Creme brûlée	Conditions
Realized	Locus tree
Wire grid	Vulnerable
Drizzle	Cherry tomato
Tapestry	Terra Cotta warrior

Article

Estimates

Especially

Subtle

Boutique

Labyrinth

Patronage

Lumberyard

Power troller

Rhetorical

Cognitive

Collaboration

Tajine

About the Author

Ginger Theisen grew up in a small town in northeast Nebraska with a strong sense of curiosity that has guided her throughout her life. Horses played a significant role starting at an early age until high school. Then her interest shifted to film as an art form inspired by the independent and foreign films she watched at the Sheldon Art Museum in Lincoln. This experience sparked her desire to pursue a career in film.

After graduating from high school in 1973, she lived in Paris and worked as an au pair, returning to the United States a year later to study film at Syracuse University in upstate New York graduating with a Bachelor's degree in Fine Arts and Film. Eventually, she got a job on the camera crew at Nebraska Educational Television (NET), a PBS affiliate. Then moved into an associate producer position in the Cultural Affairs Unit.

In late summer of 1989, she and her son moved to California where she freelanced in the San Francisco Bay area. A year later she got a job at George Lucas's visual effects company, Industrial Light and Magic (ILM). She moved through the ranks starting as a production assistant to a production coordinator and to a visual effects producer. During her fifteen years at ILM, she worked with an extraordinary talented group of people to create ground breaking visual effects on several films including *Star Wars: Episode 1 - The Phantom Menace*, *The Perfect Storm* and *A.I Artificial Intelligence*.

She left ILM in 2005 to freelance as a visual effects producer until 2012 when her career shifted to the creative side after optioning the film script *Crazy Horse* based on the life of the Lakota warrior. This prompted a move back to Nebraska to develop the film. At the same time, she worked on the Crazy Horse Ride documentary, filming the ride in June of 2013. Two months later, she traveled to Guyana with two other filmmakers to work with the Witness Project high school students to write, produce, direct and act in their first short film *Rebecca's Story*.

When she returned to Nebraska the beginning of September, work continued on the Crazy Horse Ride documentary and the feature film. A week later, she went horseback riding at Mount Michael Benedictine Abbey with one of the monks, Brother Mel. This was on September 12, 2013. They saddled up the horses and left the paddock when the horse slipped and fell, landing on top of her.

The journey through her recovery from a traumatic brain injury is in this book, bringing a sense of closure to that chapter of her life, ready to fully embrace the next chapter.